PURPOSE DRIVEN LEADERSHIP

BUILDING AND FOSTERING EFFECTIVE TEAMS

By

Brigette Tasha Hyacinth

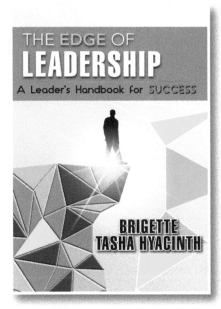

The Edge of Leadership:
A Leader's Handbook for Success

The Ultimate Leader:
Learning, Leading and Leaving a
Legacy of Hope

Dedication

First and foremost, I have to thank God for His mercies, grace, and loving kindness towards me, and for blessing me with wisdom to complete this book.

This book is dedicated to my family. I love you all so much.

My heartfelt thanks goes to my dear mother, Marguerite Joseph, who has made huge sacrifices for me to be where I am today. She is the best mother ever. She is a beautiful, loving, diligent, intelligent, and godly woman, and I am so glad to have her as my mom.

A big thank you to Frank Hyacinth, my father, and to my brothers and sisters—Troy Hyacinth, Onica Hyacinth, Gavery Enrico Hyacinth—and to Alicia Hyacinth (my sister-in-law), Che Nigel Hyacinth (deceased), Cheron Hyacinth, Ezra (Tricia) Ramlall, and Brent John for the huge support they provided.

Thank you to my nieces and nephew Nicholas Hyacinth, Celeste Hyacinth, Jessie Ramlall, Tinique Hyacinth and Sarah Davis. I am so proud of you all. May you continue to grow in the grace and knowledge of our Lord and Saviour, Jesus Christ. The world is yours for the taking. Once you put God first, nothing shall be impossible unto you. Think big, always look up, and never give up. May God richly bless you now and forevermore.

Table of Contents

PREFACE

|||||||||||||||||||||||||||||||||||||||||||||||||||||||||||||||||||||||||||||||||||||||

Everything we do in life involves teamwork in some form – family, marriage, community and work. Effective teamwork lies at the heart of success for any organization. It is the unconditional sharing of one's best skills and talents to benefit the group. To quote Aristotle, "The whole is greater than the sum of its parts." Teamwork is one of the most powerful and creative forces. It's an awesome sight to see a group of individuals working in harmony to accomplish shared goals.

This book will provide you with the strategies to build high-performing teams but it firstly requires you to work on yourself to be the leader your team needs you to be. Leaders are only as successful as the quality of the teams they have created and led. Purpose Driven Leaders recognize that the vision can only be accomplished via cooperation and collaboration so they work to build a powerhouse team that is productive, creative and efficient.

SECTION ONE

Building and Retaining High Performance Teams

CHAPTER ONE

10 INDIVIDUALS THAT MAKE UP YOUR TEAM

Leaders are inoperable without followers who are willing to accept their leadership. In particular, they need a group of individuals who are willing to learn from them as the leader and to assist in the realization of their goals. It takes great leadership to build great teams. Team building is essential in any business, however, it is easier said than done. Research states that 60% of work teams fail. You can manage machines effortlessly, but it's not the same case with people. You can't just press a button and instructions are automatically followed. Leading people brings with it lots of challenges as they have different mind-sets, values and beliefs. Expecting people to just get along is not a realistic expectation. Even the best managers experience difficulty getting everyone to cooperate. Leaders must develop a keen understanding of people, their strengths and weaknesses and what gets them motivated to work together to accomplish organizational goals. Be fully present during conversations and be observant. When you know every member's skills and their values and beliefs, you have an understanding of how they work best and will be better able to manage conflict. This information is invaluable to leaders to match each employee's expertise and competencies with the task at hand. Understanding each individual with an emphasis on how I can assist them in becoming what they want to achieve, will ultimately build trust with the individual and the team.

In research conducted with leaders in 53 countries, I have proposed 10 Types of Individuals who make up your team. If you were to randomly organize individuals in your organization and structure them into teams to work on a project, these are ten types of individuals you will **realistically** get.

10 Types of Individuals that make up your Team

1 **The Team Leader:** The initiator—they start things off. If you don't appoint someone, they will automatically take charge. They have vested leadership and act as stewards. They are the facilitators, clarifying goals and objectives and assisting to assign roles and responsibilities within the group. They guide the activities of the team to what they identify to be the team's obligations. This person has a unique ability to relate to others. They are highly perceptive and can manage internal and external relationships. They are good at getting others to work together and add humour to the group to lighten the atmosphere. They are influential collaborators and mediators. The team leader can communicate effectively with team members through good listening and verbal and non-verbal communication. They hold the fort for you and you can relax with them at the helm. However, this should not be an excuse for you to adopt a laissez-faire leadership style as you are ultimately responsible for the outcomes. Check in on them

regularly to ensure the group is going in the right direction. Yes, team leaders are dependable and reliable, but still, let them know you are the authority. I've seen cases where their leadership role went to their head, and they have tried to undermine the leader's influence which was evident in meetings and office events. It is a good idea to rotate leadership of the team regularly or within established time-frames. Regardless of whether team leaders have more observable leadership skills, rotating leadership is an excellent method to develop the leadership skills of other team members. When someone is responsible for leading a meeting or project, they will be more engaged and more aware of what is taking place in the team. Involvement leads to better teamwork. You will never have a truly high-performing team unless leadership is shared, so that everyone on the team, gets an opportunity to grow and develop.

2 **The Team Player:** They act as the team counsellor and are usually eager to help, and are very diplomatic. Team players spread positivity throughout the office. They put the company and their co-workers ahead of themselves and work to ensure the team remains united. They seek consensus. They are approachable and responsive and are aware of everyone's strengths and weaknesses on the team. Such individuals are considerate and provide support to team members by cheering them on, "yes, I think that's a good point," "that was very helpful." Members view them as trustworthy as they do not engage in gossip. They are concerned with interpersonal relationships in the group and work hard to maintain a healthy social climate. Everyone can count on them. They keep the team together, ease tensions and promote harmony. The team player is generous with their time and is not afraid to go the extra mile to help a teammate who's struggling. They are good at persuading others to jump on board. They are always volunteering and will offer to mentor the newcomers. They may be good leaders but not necessarily great

as they don't want to rock the boat and are concerned about how others think of them. They typically don't want to be the boss. Don't assume they can do everything although they are always ready and willing. Don't always ask too much from them because they can't say no. Keep their motivation high always.

3 | **The Proficient:** They are excellent at what they do and are quite knowledgeable. They are continuous learners and keep abreast with what is going on in the environment. They will provide you with critical updates. If you are heading to a meeting and you need to clarify some information you can always look to them. This person creates innovative solutions. They don't just think outside the box, they think about where the box originated, why it's currently positioned there and how the design could be improved. They commend good ideas and reject bad ones. They may make others in the group feel "not so smart" so advise them to don't shoot down other individual's ideas as they may come across as arrogant or this may reduce feedback.

4 | **The Achiever: The Go-getter.** They are concerned about getting things done and relish challenges. They are action and results-oriented. They are creative and come up with bright ideas. They often have strategies for improving a process or increasing team efficiency. They are task-oriented and push the team to set high-performance standards and to use their resources wisely. These individuals develop a plan of execution based upon the goals of the company. If the team is moving at a slow pace, they will be anxious about deadlines and targets. They want the team to do well because they know the team performance can negatively or positively affect their individual performance rating. They volunteer to find out certain information and give the team its drive and momentum. Achievers are high-energy and very driven individuals. They can be over zealous, so you might have to let them know we need to get all the facts before we can spearhead

17

a decision. They are naturally self-motivated so keep in mind their career progression and give them more responsibility inclusive of stretch goals. They are talented, enthusiastic and confident. Once it's proven, there are no opportunities for growth and development; they will plan an exit strategy and eventually leave the organization (*job-hopping*). These individuals along with Apprentices form the highest turnover rates of the organization.

5 **The Freeloader:** These individuals don't pull their weight and are always distracting the team. They have the highest absenteeism and poorest punctuality rates. You can't depend on them. If you give them an assignment, they will show up late for the presentation or say they forgot their role. They have an excuse for everything and are always eager to recommend someone who is better for the task. Adopt an assertive attitude in dealing with them. Have a candid discussion with them to align organizational objectives with their career aspirations into a perfect fit. Set them goals with deadlines and monitor the progress. Make them accountable for the team result. Due to continuous poor performance, and after every opportunity has been given to them to improve their performance, they are the most likely to be asked to leave the organization.

6 | **The Militant:** They challenge assumptions. They are always giving reasons why something is not feasible, or it won't work. They are useful to prevent groupthink as they critically evaluate and analyze the proposals, ideas, and contributions of others in the team. They dig deep and are reluctant to take things at face value. However, they cause unnecessary delays in meetings because they require explanations. You always have to justify why a certain course of action is being taken. They are outspoken and make sure their voice is heard. You need to understand the reasons behind their behaviour. Some are genuinely interested in getting to the facts, and they want the group to think critically by steering them in the right direction while others are merely critics. Facing them is like going into a battle. They get satisfaction in finding fault. You have to prepare yourself mentally to deal with them; don't get confrontational, respond don't react and take control of the conversation as needed. They are inflexible and often argumentative, and this may cause friction in the group. One way to get people who don't agree with a decision is to give them a leadership role. You can enlist militants in risk mitigation. Ask them to take responsibility for finding a way to mitigate their top concerns.

7 **The Veteran:** Those who have been in the organization for a long time and know the ropes. They always let others know about their length of tenure in the organization and what works and what doesn't. They gave a lot of examples of organizational history. Some of them are team players while others have become disgruntled or disengaged and have been reduced to spectators, just observing everything on the sidelines. Their philosophy is "been there, done that, it doesn't lead anywhere." They may not care to contribute as they have continually been overlooked for internal vacancies or promotions. Don't throw your long- standing Veterans under the bus. Make them feel appreciated and give them the respect they desire and deserve. They have given a lifetime of service to the company. Some of the Apprentices were not even born when they started employment with the organization. They still are a tremendous asset to the organization. Not all people with great ideas have degrees or work in the more glamorous positions; their inputs are based on real world experience which can be far more valuable than a degree and no experience. A wise leader will leverage their experience and recommend continuous learning to them. Learning new systems and processes may be difficult for them as some prefer to cling to outdated methods than to embrace change and innovation. Give them support and all opportunities for them to update their skills.

8 **The Apprentice**—The Newcomer. They are inexperienced. Some of them may take a back seat as they absorb everything; trying to come on stream. Others are eager to indicate their academic qualifications and to give a fresh perspective. They often will agree with proposed plans because they don't want to make waves or be termed a 'troublemaker.' So even if they don't agree, they just go with the flow. Provide training, coaching and mentoring. It's easier to get them to conform to organizational culture in this early stage. Work closely with them as they

are impressionable. You don't want the cynical militants and disgruntled veterans to negatively influence their perspective about building a future in the company.

9 The **Wisenheimer**—The Know-it-all. They feel it necessary to share every opinion. They see themselves as the go-to person. If there's a problem, they have the solution; if there's a question, they have the answer. They talk the most and interrupt others. They come across as self-centred. They tend to monopolize conversations and are dismissive of others' opinions. They always have to interject to correct others. Unfortunately, this forces other team members to keep quiet, even if they have what they believe to be a good idea. The team secretly view them as annoying. A lot of their contributions may lack relevance or may not be based on facts. They will carry everyone around in circles to end up at the same point. Most of the team are reluctant to challenge them because you can't win an argument with them. It's difficult to get through to them. Their belief that they can do no wrong makes them poorly receptive to constructive criticism. You may respond to their point by saying, "Christopher, Thank you for your comments and I've recorded them for future discussion but in respect of time and our agreed-upon agenda, let's move on." You can also sign them up to attend training sessions on effective communication techniques. Timely intervention is necessary. Sometimes it is important to make them realize that their behaviour is having a negative effect on the rest of the team. Sadly though, they may view this a personal attack on them because management is jealous that they know more than them.

10 **Individualist** —This person is independent and self-reliant. They keep to themselves and shun group building activities. If you organize an event offsite, they mostly will not attend unless it's compulsory. Most of the team know little information about

them. They are quiet and reserved but very observant. They mainly provide feedback when called upon or prompted to do so. Some Individualists are introverts and have a hard time socializing with the group while others are simply self-seeking. They prefer to work on their own. This could have stemmed from a past negative experience in group settings. In this technology age, we see a trend in society towards individualism. Starting from the home, family members no longer gather together or engage in conversation to the extent in previous years since everyone is absorbed on some technological gadget or on the television. **As leaders we need to get people to communicate, collaborate and cooperate**. Many individuals can chat and text for hours on social media but when they meet face-to-face, they find it difficult to connect with others. Gradually push Individualists to participate in team building activities that would build their trust and confidence and align them to teams where collaboration is mandatory.

It should be noted that some personalities overlap, and sometimes you'll find one person plays more than one role. A recent study conducted by the Kellogg School of Management found that in a typical six-to-eight person meeting, three people do 70% of the talking. As well as early ideas tend to have disproportionate influence over the rest of the conversation. One of the researchers, Professor Leigh Thompson, explained that the dominant people don't often realize that they're doing most of the talking. "In fact," she says, "they vehemently argue that meetings are egalitarian." Working on a team with different personalities and skill sets can be challenging. As the leader, you should analyse team dynamics to make the most of the human assets at your disposal. Firstly, by understanding each group member and how their behaviour changes within the team, and secondly, how individual responses vary at different stages of the team's development. Concentrating on the nature and the quality of the relations between team members is key in team achievements. Therefore encourage all members of the team to speak in meetings. When teams invite everyone on the team to contribute, team intelligence goes up. Don't just lean on one person or the loudest voice. Get everyone involved. For example, *«We haven›t heard from some of you yet, so I encourage you to share your ideas, questions, and suggestions.»* *"Your input is valuable".* If necessary, call on them: "Sarah, I know you had great success with your cost projection. Can you share some tips with us." Teams make better decisions when everyone contributes and feels comfortable doing so. Different personality types communicate in different ways. Learn how people like to contribute and focus on their strengths. Learn who prefers to contribute in the background and who likes being in the spotlight. Don't look down on a team member who may not be particularly vocal in the group setting, but who later on will approach you separately with their ideas. When you build trust with your team, know the values and goals of each person, as well as what they need from you as their leader, you will be better able to get the best out of each member of your team.

CHAPTER TWO

HOW TO BUILD A STRONG TEAM

Leadership is the art of getting someone else to do something you want done because he wants to do it. —Dwight Eisenhower

To compete in today's changing market landscape, organizations need strong, adaptable and creative teams that thrive in uncertain environments. Can a business achieve success without its employees cooperating effectively as a team? It is crucial that companies build teams of highly motivated individuals that work together smoothly to bring about success. All successful leaders have a great team at their core. Great leaders understand that they are only as good as their weakest link, so they work to build a powerhouse team that is efficient and productive. Most organizations know the importance of building and fostering teams, but building an effective team requires ongoing commitment and input from leaders. It may take one person with a vision to get a business started, but if you don't focus on building a strong team, you can't achieve sustainable success. Your business is only as effective as your team.

Larger groups frequently have a hard time maintaining teamwork and unity of purpose. For breakthrough results, sometimes small is better. With a small team, tasks stay focused, there are fewer conflicts as everyone knows everyone which is a must for a cohesive team. Additionally, adopt situational leadership to enhance your team's effectiveness. Remember, there is no one-size-fits-all approach in teambuilding. The leadership team must be aligned and committed to the vision and strategy. If not, personal conflicting agendas may be pursued which could be costly to the organization.

Don't let your team be a victim of poor planning. Before you get started, chart all of these upcoming considerations out and open the floor for discussions. Effective team building can be challenging at first. Take the time to identify your goals and create a plan. Make sure sufficient time is allocated appropriately for team-building activities. Establish a set of values for acceptable methods and behaviours. It is important for leaders to cultivate a spirit of generosity, empathy and diplomacy. Set up and uphold the rules of engagement, interaction and conduct. Lead by example; your team members will look to you for guidance and inspiration. If you expect high productivity and quality work, it's important that you do it in the same way. The leader should be able to discern when the team needs external assistance. Bring in experts as needed. You need to be aware of limits to existing team capabilities and accept that seeking help externally under the right conditions is a sign of strength rather than weakness. Some challenges go deeper or broader than the specific tasks usually addressed. Cross-functional teams can help break down systemic operational issues. If you do have a large team and a complicated project, consider adding one of the team members as the lead on the project. The team leader is the person to keep in touch with fellow team members and to make sure everything is on schedule. Although it is likely that the leadership role will shift from one team member to another (determined by task demands and skills), the fact remains that there is usually a team leader responsible for reporting the outcomes from his/her team's performance. To ensure that team leaders are actively engaging employees, provide them with coaching. Formal training on team leadership can dramatically improve the effectiveness of team leaders. This will give them the support they may need in carrying out their duties.

A leader should have an understanding of 'group dynamics' Groups go through various stages as they develop to effective team working. A common model used to track the development of groups was suggested by Bruce Tuckman in 1965 which outlines four stages of team development:

> **Forming** - The team meets and learns and agree on goals and begins to tackle the tasks. Team members tend to behave quite independently. They attempt to become oriented to the tasks and with each other.

> **Storming** - Disagreements and personality clashes occur at this stage. Tolerance of each team member and their

differences should be emphasized; without tolerance and patience, the team will fail. Teach positive conflict management. Knowing how to turn conflict into a positive is desirable but does not come easily. Conflict is inevitable, but a team that values one another's strengths and respectfully communicates with each other will use conflict as an opportunity for growth and even greater success. The team must work on resolutions, not on retribution aimed at others. Inability to properly handle conflict can lead to a team making little or no progress.

> **Norming** - At this stage the group is beginning to work through its conflicts and agree on ways of functioning towards actual performance.

> **Performing** - With group norms and roles established, group members focus on objectives. Now the team is working together towards a common goal. This foundation is built by establishing trust among team members.

All teams will develop at different rates, and some may get caught in one of the phases. The important thing is to be aware of the complex dynamics of the group development process. Although subtle, there are differences between groups and teams. All teams are groups of individuals, but not all groups are teams. A group is a collection of individuals forming a unit for a reason or cause whereas a team is a collection of individuals sharing a common goal and acting towards it. The difference primarily lies in the direction of action. A group can exist and yet not accomplish anything. A team, on the other hand, is results-oriented. It has a clear purpose which is shared by its members. A team works together and shares the results, while a group is more independent of each other. Without purpose and goals, you cannot build a team. In a strong team, members share a high level of commitment to achieving the common objectives and experience a high level of satisfaction from being part of and working with the team.

A strong team starts with effective leadership. Know your team and form relationships with employees not only on a professional level but also on a personal level. By getting to individually know your team and what motivates them, you will have a better chance of building an efficient team. Management needs an open-door policy to keep communication flowing freely. The manager must be on the floor, working alongside the team. You must be available. If you work behind closed doors, you are promoting uncooperative work. However, building a collaborative culture starts with you. Team members need to feel that they can approach management whenever necessary to keep the project running smoothly especially when issues arise, that they cannot resolve on their own. Pay attention to conflicts when they occur. Don't turn a blind eye as this will make the atmosphere more toxic. When any confrontation happens, listen to all sides carefully and address the situation on an urgent basis, act as the mediator. Work out ways to resolve conflicts. What works as an effective style of conflict resolution varies from team to team, and may vary over time on the same team. It's natural for conflict to arise when people work in groups.

10 Steps to Build an Effective Team

1. **Select the right people.** This is critical. You want the most talented people, but only those who are willing to work together for the team's success. The health of the organization requires the proper use of the skills possessed by each member. A strong team is comprised of individuals with a variety of skills and backgrounds, which produces a healthy level of diversity within the team. The focus sometimes is on hiring individuals for short-term needs, when the long-term objective of developing strong teams is what creates organizational sustainability. Technical skills for a role are essential and easy to measure but traits such as "team player" and self-awareness are better predictors of long-term success and are harder to evaluate. For a team to be able to effective, its members must display the range of skills, knowledge and experience for the task it is undertaking. Selecting the right people to be on the team is crucial. Human Resources (HR) selection processes should be streamlined to discover at the onset during the interviewing process, whether candidates are a right fit. When selecting an individual for a team, discuss their experiences to get a sense of how he or she operated within a team. When inquiring about team-based successes, does the individual emphasize his or her role in achieving success, or is credit shared with others? A toxic or non-compliant member on the team can bring an organization to its knees if left unaddressed. **The 20-80 principle advocates that 20 percent of the people you have to deal with produce 80 percent of the problems.** Ask many leaders what their experience is, and you will find them in agreement. Most

of management will confess that a relatively small percentage of their employees give them the most resistance. Unfortunately, not all people would like to conform as we would prefer them to. Some people provide a serious challenge to our leadership function. Management can eliminate problem personnel right from the start in this method. Questioning the job candidate and having him or her site examples to assess if he/she works well with others and understands the importance of teamwork is an effective way to accomplish this. Their philosophy must be as the famous quote by John F. Kennedy's in his inaugural address goes "ask not what your country can do for you, ask what you can do for your country."

"The bigger the dream, the more important the team." — Robin Sharma

A group of highly skilled employees working together does not guarantee a successful team. You don't need your team members to be great at everything. In fact, you probably only need them to be great at one thing. Hire the best and leverage the strengths of others to create an extraordinary team. Select talented individuals with a passion for performing and a strong work ethic. You can teach a skill, but you can't teach ingenuity or drive. *They must be committed to the team*: their principal concern is with the best interest of the team and its performance at heart. This will ensure projects are done well and within stipulated deadlines. Choose your employees wisely with respect to how willing they give their all to their job. Passionate people fuel incredible energy. They spare little thought for the rewards; they're absorbed in overcoming the challenges and finding solutions. There's nothing like the focus and creativity of a team of committed and talented individuals, willing to put the team's success ahead of their personal goals to deliver the seemingly impossible. Leadership of the team and the people that you hire make a significant difference to your success. Some characteristics of a high performing team member include strong personal drive and work ethic, capacity to remain adaptable, an ability to exhibit humility and a willingness to learn from others.

2 | Communication of shared vision and clear purpose. The purpose must be meaningful and create a sense of doing something significant together. If people are confused as to what the organization is trying to accomplish and their role, it's unlikely you'll realize the true potential of your people. If you want to get somewhere, you have to know where you are going and the path you are willing to take. This will serve as your guide in hiring, and your team's true compass once you are up and running. Clarity of vision_will serve to motivate every team member and keep them focused on the attainment of goals. The organization must be clear as to why it exists-mission and where it is heading-vision. People need to connect with the mission and be inspired by the vision before they can fully engage. Most companies have a great mission, and vision statements but how many employees know what these statements are or actually mean? Do your people understand the mission and vision and are they inspired to give their best to achieve it? For example, my organization's mission is "To improve the competence of leaders and their organisations." Therefore, if ever there is a question of what to do in a given situation, employees at any level can make the right decision based on answering that question.

Every team is working together to achieve some manner of success. Sadly, though they are not always clear on what success is. For a team to be successful there must be a clear, agreed definition of what success is. A 2011 study conducted by, Shteynberg and Galinsky (2011) reported findings that "participants pursued goals more intensely when they were aware that others were experiencing the same individual goal."

Teams thrive when there is a clear direction. Include your team in creating team goals and values, so they know what is required and they agree to it. It is necessary to clarify the team's performance goals and to explain how the team contributes to the overall success of the organization. The leader has a crucial role in communicating a clear vision of what the organization expects from the team. You need to encourage your employees to take ownership of the team's work. There must be a commitment to a common purpose. The more collaboration and teamwork that you do, the more benefits your customer will have with the end product. Put team members in touch with the people who use your product or service. Bring the customers in, get their feedback and then share that with the organization. Confirm the needs of the customers or clients on an ongoing basis so relevant improvements can be made. Knowledge is power. When everyone in the organization is aware of the customers' needs, wants and issues, it promotes unity. A unified team is one in which everyone works together toward common goals. A combination of both task and relationship functions are necessary for effective team performance.

3 | **Strategy and Goals must be clear** – What is your competitive advantage? You need to focus on and develop this area of expertise. Your competitive advantage needs to be determined before you decide the strategies required to leverage your strengths in the marketplace. Your team should be acutely aware of this edge so they can invest their time and energy wisely. If people are working on the insignificant things, they will just be running in circles. Strategies must align or connect to a clear vision. Your people need to participate in developing strategies as this promotes the buy-in approach. Leadership needs to clearly articulate the strategies and communicate at all levels so everyone can see how they fit into the big picture. Employees that buy into the strategies will be more engaged and deliver

more value. They must have clear direction, competitive edge and a strategy, to be empowered to produce something that has value in the marketplace.

Building an efficient team involves setting clear and S.M.A.R.T. (Specific, Measurable, Attainable, Realistic and Timely) goals for the team to meet. The team's overall objective needs to be identified and defined which allow each member to have the same purpose. For team building to be effective, members must have the same aims for being on the team. The goals must be specific and challenging so that each member can understand how they contribute to the success of the team. There has to be an end result that everyone is working toward. It's not only important to make sure that the goals are clarified; you also want to make sure that each team member is working towards the same end result. If someone on your team has a different goal, they should be reassigned to a different team.

Clarify each person's role in achieving the common goal. Promote Skills: Each team member has a different and unique set of competencies. Ensure everyone knows their place in the team. Assess what their strengths are and assign them to the appropriate task as per their strengths and competencies. Align the right roles with the right talent. Your team members will work better and be more engaged and satisfied when they feel, that their skills are being suitably utilized. This will significantly impact on the output of your team. Get people working on their strengths and have others support them on their weaker areas- this is what teamwork is all about. You're only as strong as your weakest link. You need to assess your current team and understand who the "C" players are and work with them to get them to understand what it takes to become an "A" player. Define each person's task in terms of their contribution to the team's goals and the overall organization's goals. This will eliminate any differences of opinions and views among the team as responsibilities are clearly defined. Give your employees flexibility on how to meet their work goals. Encourage them to make suggestions about changes based on their direct and daily experience of what works, what doesn't work, and what could be improved.

Conductor and composer Leonard Bernstein once was asked: "Mister Bernstein, which is the most difficult instrument?" Bernstein replied: "The second violin. I can get many first violinists, but to find one who with the same enthusiasm plays second violin or second French horn or second flute, is a real problem. Yet, if nobody would play second violin, we would not have harmony." It is not always easy to be second, especially if one wants to be first. Team members must show self-sacrifice and humility knowing it's not about them but the success of the team as a whole.

4 **Maintain good communication for building trust and respect.** Communication is key. Make sure everyone is on the same page. Be transparent as this builds trust between you and the team. An atmosphere which encourages a questioning approach is likely to reveal any members' reservations, misunderstandings or resistances which need to be positively remedied. A quality team must have the ability to accurately perceive what is happening. The group needs to be able to identify issues. Ensure that your team has access to the required information to complete their tasks. The team should be 'up to date' of all changes, challenges and successes. Employees want to know all information surrounding the project, so it's crucial that you provide the details with your team members on a consistent basis. It will motivate them to deliver their best. It's important to discuss what's already been accomplished and describe problems the team is experiencing. Regular meetings with team members is an easy way to encourage effective communication. Listen and respond to feedback. Offer constructive feedback that is positive and productive which acknowledges both what works

and what doesn't work. This helps improve performance and the end results. One of the main reasons projects fail is due to lack of communication. Encourage members of the team to voice their ideas and suggestions. The team could have the answers to particular problems management discovers. Feedback from them can often lead to operations running more efficiently. Maintaining good communication with your team will make you accessible, which will increase the trust and respect within your team.

5 | **Foster a strong company culture** - Create an inspiring working environment. Set a culture of "Listening to Learn." I see so many teams wasting time just touching the surface of an issue then to realize they didn't get to the root cause which was apparent only if they had listened more. Lead from the front rather than pushing them from behind. Be an example. Create a good working environment for the team. Change the verbal language. Replace "I" and "you" with "we" and "us. Create a 'Can do attitude'. Culture connects employees to and gives them a sense of belonging which can create emotional bonding thus strengthening and improving team efforts. That's the intangible team spirit that makes your team feel part of something worthwhile. Set the kind of climate conducive to optimal performance. Dispel any apprehensions and fears among your team members. Cultivate a healthy organization for employees to contribute their best. Constantly inspire them about the possibilities to execute the vision effectively. Enlighten them to look ahead at the door that is opened, not the ones that are closed. Working in a team means taking a constructive, can-do approach. Help your team keep a clear mind and focus. Ask questions to provide guidance; questions that will allow employees to brainstorm the solution and take responsibility to correct the issue. "How would you recommend we approach this issue? "What steps should we take to avoid this from reoccurring?"

Align their energies and efforts towards organizational goals continuously; this will reduce delays and detours caused by distractions. To maximize productivity, take care of your team's day-to-day concerns. As Robin Sharma stated, "Assets are not time plus money, but energy plus focus." The emphasis is on strengths and on the positive. Remove barriers. Ensure the right practices are in place for each team member to deliver their full potential and help and encourage them every step of the way. Additionally, keep promises. Make sure you support your team to achieve the required results.

Create an environment that encourages vulnerability. It's very difficult for a team to come together with walls of silence built up in between them. One of the best things any leader can do is create an environment that allows for openness. Everyone has weaknesses, and if they verbalize them in an atmosphere that promotes vulnerability, it encourages teamwork instead of divisiveness. Be consistent. You must be intentional and committed. People must see that changes aren't temporary but part of an ongoing process. The more recommended changes are implemented, the more people would be motivated to participate knowing their efforts don't fall on deaf ears. Doing so improves employee satisfaction and elevates productivity.

6 | Encourage teamwork – **Train for Teamwork**. Send your team to a seminar or workshop on team building; send them together, if possible. Support an environment of collaboration. ClearCompany.com states that 86% of employees and executives cite a lack of collaboration or ineffective communication for workplace failures (Salesforce says this percentage can be as high as 96%). Help your team effectively work together by urging them to share information and resources among themselves. Encourage them to work with one another, by pairing them and requiring that they complete a specific task together.

Mentoring is a fantastic way to facilitate this as those who are more experienced help to guide those who may be newer to the role or organization. New staff members can be paired with team members who have more exposure. The goal of every mentor is to help mentees at all levels grow in their respective positions. New team members are quickly integrated into the team. It's important to foster open communication and help them learn how to work together. Learning how to communicate to better collaborate is crucial. If we understand how others need to receive information and feedback, we become a more effective team.

Team members need to invest time and effort into developing working techniques to move the team toward its goal in the most efficient way. These include methods for making decisions and solving problems. There must be mutual respect and a willingness to help each other. Joint problem solving must be adopted and the tendency to 'blame others' is supplanted with focus on understanding problems and finding solutions. It's important to recognize if team members mainly address their questions and suggestions to you, or do they interact directly with each other at meetings. Encourage feedback from individual team members. This will help the team members to come up with any issue they want to address. Conversations must take place in which everyone listens and feels free to respond in turn. The readiness of all team members to communicate ideas and concerns is important to the overall success of any project. No idea must be seen as "stupid" or any contribution as menial. Team members should approach all conversations with respect and honesty. Recommend team members ask each other for help and to offer it to each other, without feeding it all through you. The order of the day is participation and personal responsibility. Members are encouraged to contribute ideas and question the team and its activities openly without fear of censorship or condemnation.

Delegate authority. Let your team members take responsibility for the project. Ownership is what makes people feel they are a critical part of the team. This requires considerable flexibility on your part but allows other team members to exercise real leadership. Share responsibility with others who are better skilled in certain areas of the business than you are. You won't always have control of all changes in your business so learn to trust others and support their decisions. Trust your team - Trust them that they will do the right thing, and in return, they will trust you by focusing their efforts on the project rather than worrying about you breathing down their necks. Don't micromanage. Let them know "I trust your decisions... or I trust that you can..." If you find that you do have to micromanage your team, then it's time to find new team members. Part of the joy of team building is the freedom you have to let go and trust that they'll lead themselves. Each project that is completed and each team that you build is a source of information on how to continue to grow and improve your results.

7 **Support innovation and invest in learning.** Creative thinking involves risk. Members should be adept at brainstorming ideas and willing to transform routine processes to make them more efficient. Remove the roadblocks of the people you serve, and they will take you further than you imagine. Give your team avenues and time to share ideas and think about their projects offsite. Listen to their problems and facilitate solutions. When problems arise, encourage team members to be solution focused rather than problem focused. Problems should be analyzed for what they can contribute to the collective learning process. Focus on solving problems and not pinpointing individuals. When a problem occurs try to get to the source of it to solve it; the worst you can do is start finger pointing. This will unravel any bond that has been formed. Constructive criticism is intended to help the team and its members to increase their efficacy.

This allows for coaching and mentoring. Mentor and guide them and spend time with them. Provide support for them to understand and correct their mistakes. Inspire forward thinking; encourage team members to consider how a suggested solution to any given problem serves the organization's goals and how it will impact those goals. The organizational structure and infrastructure should be developed to enable the achievement of a vision through the agreed upon strategies. Your team needs to be organized in a way that allows their creativity to flow. Many organizational structures are outdated or bureaucratic. Too often, the methods for implementing great ideas are far too complex.

To be able to use the full potential of innovation, psychological safety within teams and organisations is essential. Psychological safety is the shared belief that it is safe within the team for interpersonal risk taking. There is a direct relation between a psychological safe climate and performance of the team. (Edmondson 1999)

An environment has to be created that enables intentional success, and everyone needs to do their part to achieve the desired results. Give them the space to innovate, to be able to make mistakes and start over. In 1989, Steve Jobs had already pointed out the importance of the right team during an interview for Fortune Magazine: "Innovation has nothing to do with how many Research and Development (R&D) dollars you have. When Apple came up with the Mac, IBM was spending at least 100 times more on R&D. It's not about money. It's about the people you have, how you're led, and how much you get it." Thinking-out-of-the box is what you need from the team members. A bumblebee dropped into an open glass tumbler will stay there until it dies. It never sees the means of its escape from above but persists in trying to find some other way out through the sides. People are excited motivated to work for an organization where their professional and personal aspirations can be fulfilled. Give them the scope of the project and autonomy to execute tasks. The acceptance of trial and error opens the door of ingenuity which leads to innovation and growth. Create an environment where failure or saying "I don't know" is not seen as a weakness. The ability to be honest and open will strengthen your team's cohesiveness. Empower your team members. Allow them to explore and experiment. A leader who can provide the right amount of room for experimentation can awaken the power of creativity. When your team feel a sense of freedom, they will come up with some great ideas. If they fail, ask them to incorporate the lessons learned from failures to keep moving forward.

"It doesn't make sense to hire *smart people* and then *tell them* what to do; we hire *smart people* so they can *tell* us what to do." —*Steve Jobs.*

In building a strong team and company culture, change will be inevitable. Changes can centre on systems or processes or equipment that need upgrading. Be transparent when going through change. Let your team know the impact it will have on the organization and them on a personal level. Furthermore, **invest in learning.** Provide team members with the opportunity to learn, grow and undertake work they find meaningful and rewarding. Understand that the team's growth is your growth which is the organizations' growth. Nurturing a culture of innovative thinkers takes advantage of the shared knowledge and experience of everyone in the company. It also helps to bring natural leaders to the forefront whose skills can then be better utilized within the business. Support professional development through appropriate conferences, training workshops, and seminars. This will help them develop their abilities while enabling them to make a greater contribution to the company. They will become more valuable to you, the team, and the organization.

8 | **Treat your people right. Demonstrate that you value people.** If we are selfish, rude and unsympathetic; if we treat people only as the means to an end, if we keep trampling on others in an attempt to advance ourselves, this will lead to low morale. Members must feel valued for what they can and have contributed. If you treat your team right, they will be eager to invest considerable energy in the interests of the team. Treat them as contributors and respect them. If people genuinely believe in who they are following, **t**rust will follow. Team members should not feel any pressure or intimidated to come directly to you. A survey, from the American Psychological Association, found that feeling valued plays a key role in an employee's decision to either stay or leave his or her present employer. It can also have a positive effect on their motivation, job satisfaction and engagement. In contrast, 50 percent of the participants who felt undervalued conveyed that they would be searching for new employment opportunities within the next year. How do you maintain the motivation of any team? Lots of genuine concern. Lots of listening. Lots of "Thank Yous." I want everyone on my team to succeed both professionally and personally. Take a genuine interest in your team. Encourage them to have lives outside of work. If you always work them at 110%, you will burn them out especially when you need them to be on top of their game. You ultimately want good team spirit to abound. Yes, success is vital, but you still want members to feel good about their team and to be confident and motivated. They should feel proud and inspired.

"Employees who believe that management is concerned about them as a whole person – not just an employee – are more productive, more satisfied, more fulfilled. Satisfied employees mean satisfied customers, which leads to profitability." —Anne M. Mulcahy

9 Assess and Evaluate Team Building Success and Recognize and Reward. You want to make sure that the steps you are taking are generating the most return on investment. This means implementing systems to assess progress and success and to evaluate results. Set performance targets and milestones and establish ways in which the team's movement toward achieving the goals can be measured. It should be decided early on what measures will be used to assess progress and how often will performance reviews of the team as a whole be performed. The advantage of defining how progress will be measured is that team members will be able to assess themselves. An effective team recognizes the importance of monitoring the team itself and are accountable for the results produced. It is important that performance targets are challenging without being impractical. When the right performance standards are established, the team's energy is directed towards accomplishing goals. Team performance must be continually appraised, in order to identify any problems experienced by members. Teams experience failure; Teams experience success - Take both in good stride. Remember everyone is watching your response to deem what is acceptable and what isn't. A leader who takes full credit for the team's work won't have an engaged team for very long. When you have great team members, reward them for their efforts and successes. Appreciate the team and individuals for good work. Everyone needs to be acknowledged in the same manner for their role on the team. Look at your metrics in monthly reporting and reinforce what behaviours are acceptable. Give your team small perks or bigger ones as budget permits. Recognize and reward staff in ways that suit their personality. Rewards can be monetary, but people also appreciate recognition. Some

members may prefer open praise while others may only want tangible rewards. When the leader talks about accomplishments, every single team member should be acknowledged by name. Employees work more productively when their work is valued, recognized and appreciated. It's essential to appraise and reward the team as a whole. Compare the team's performance to what was expected. Give more attention and place more emphasis on team performance rather than just individual performance to always promote the foundation of teamwork.

10 **Work Hard, Play Hard (Celebrate):** Create opportunities and allow time for team members to interact at a personal level. Spend time building relationships and fostering trust. Arrange fun activities as a team that will strengthen relationships between employees. There is a well-known saying that there is no 'I' in team, but the reality is that a team is full of individuals. Each person has their own objectives, values and beliefs. They also have unique talents. To work effectively as a team, it's important for everyone to get to know one another. You need to get a good understanding of each other; from values, goals and competencies. This deeper level of understanding makes it easier to work together. Develop team-building activities and games. Some of these may be better suitable off-site to encourage a more relaxed atmosphere where everyone can be themselves. This will help to strengthen the bond as a team. Socializing helps team members get to know one another better so they can anticipate everyone's actions and needs on the project. Organize company retreats: it is not only advisable to revisit company goals, but also share personal goals as well in this environment. Sharing goals helps your team to connect with each other and to look past any tension that may occur during the normal day-to-day operations. Have fun. A team that plays together stays together. Examine the way your team works together and try to improve communication and cooperation. Celebrate victories.

Plan small celebrations for the team for achieving important milestones. If you don't take the time to acknowledge a job well done, after a while your team will slowly fragment as they see no point in giving you their all. Treat the team as a family: Share the happiness and disappointments together. Add humour. This is a great way to reduce status distinctions and to make your team feel more comfortable around you. Humour can also help to reduce stress. Four hundred years ago, Robert Burton, in his Anatomy of Melancholy, cited authorities who said, "Humour purges the blood, making the body lively and fit for any manner of employment." The German philosopher Immanuel Kant believed a hearty laugh to be "a good way to jog internally without going outdoors."

HOW TO AVOID GROUPTHINK

Sometimes, the spirit of teamwork can also be the root of its ruin. Tight- knit teams with a strong spirit of cooperation and cohesion can also generate a feeling of invulnerability and a tendency to reject suggestions and recommendations that contradict popular points, as well as shunning anybody who disagrees. The problem for the successful group is one of complacency. The overriding pursuit of consensus above all other priorities develops as the tendency to conform and adhere to the group. The team's success and cohesion become their worst enemy. Groupthink occurs when members of a group yield to consensus or the most vocal members and fail to consider all the potential options and consequences. Groupthink is a term first used in 1972 by social psychologist Irving L. Janis and is often tied to poor decisions that arise out of teams or groups. A study by Ryerson University published in the European Management Journal finds that despite past beliefs that "group cohesion" can not only help a team's performance, it can also have a downside:

groupthink. Sean Wise, professor of entrepreneurship at Ryerson, conducted a study of more than 180 teams at a national travel agency. Wise concluded that while social connections boosted a team's performance at first, too much cohesion eventually led to diminished performance. "Too much of a good thing can backfire over time... overly friendly teams lapse into groupthink, inhibiting their pursuit of new ideas and strategies."

Make sure there is room for diverse views. Teams can easily slip into group think, especially when they are successful. **Embrace Diversity;** when everyone approves and has the same background or experience, you're left with groupthink. Opinions will go unchallenged; ideas will go unquestioned, and generally you form a team of sycophants who do not care to innovate or identify problems because they are quite comfortable with the status quo. Those who see defects in the way the group operates, or who see improvements may be politely ignored or even treated with hostility. Teams, guilty of this can fail when their environment changes and they don't adapt. Create a culture that fosters creative conflict where employees are encouraged to critically analyze situations thus ensuring a full understanding of all decisions, consequences and options. Conflict within teams can be good. Conflict handled well, can produce constructive ideas. In fact, it is arguably the hallmark of a great team. Set boundaries which are flexible enough to give permission for people to run hard and fast and make decisions that are outside the norm. Opposing opinions, suggestions and feedback are to be welcomed. **Assign a "devil's advocate."** to ensure all sides of a topic are discussed. Inquiring into views that may not have been spoken can allow better team performance. By asking the team, "What else do we need to consider here?" Effective leaders build team trust by encouraging a diversity of opinion. Always ask for and encourage mixed viewpoints. Finally, it may be time to rotate team members who regularly work with and are comfortable with each other if groupthink has become uncontrollable.

Remote / Virtual / Dispersed Teams

Thirty-seven percent of U.S. workers say they have telecommuted, with the average worker logging in remotely at least two days per month. These results are based on Gallup's annual Work and Education poll, conducted in August 2015. According to infographic from Highfive, there was a **79.7% increase** in the number of remote workers between 2005 and 2012, and that number just keeps jumping higher today. A study by Forester Research predicted that about 63 million people, (43 percent of the U.S workforce) would telecommute in 2016. This is 29 million more than the figure it had in 2009. Additionally, Accenture predicts that 43% of the US workforce will be freelancers by 2020 working from multiple locations across multiple clients. In the UK freelancers alone makeup around 40 percent of the entire self-employed population, contributing £109 billion to the UK economy every year. Deloitte reports that only

12% of the executives they contacted feel they understand the way people work together in networks. Connecting with, motivating, and holding a remote workforce accountable brings unique challenges for leaders. 65% of remote employees report that they have never had a team building session. Successful virtual team players all have a few things in common: good communication skills, high emotional intelligence and an ability to work independently. In their seminal 2001 study of 70 such groups, professors Vijay Govindarajan and Anil Gupta found that 82% fell short of their goals and 33% rated themselves as largely unsuccessful. A 2005 Deloitte study of IT projects outsourced to virtual work groups found that 66% failed to satisfy the clients' requirements.

Strategies for building team effectiveness in remote employee groups

> **Encourage communication.** Use technology wisely. Promote ongoing communication by video conferencing and simple check-ins—which will help increase employee satisfaction. Open a chat room and leave it perpetually open to boost team spirit. It will foster better working relationships between the team, and they will not feel as if they are working separately but are truly a part of the organization. **Get face time**; your remote team needs face time with managers and colleagues at regular intervals to ensure closer collaboration, fostering personal connections and getting feedback. Remote team members don't have a chance to rub elbows at the photocopy machine or lean over a cubicle for some idle chat. *So* don't cut the Chit-Chat. Your kick-off meetings should have an icebreaker at the start to engage team members. Try to spend a couple of minutes at the onset of each meeting discussing personal updates.

- **Empower your Team**. For teams that rarely meet face-to-face, empowerment is critical for performance. Every team needs defined roles, a clear task strategy and interaction norms. Discuss together how the team wishes to provide feedback, hold each other accountable and works best. Remote work does come with a degree of flexibility but leaders should set clear expectations while still giving a degree of autonomy. Determine how conflicts will be resolved. Clashes in a virtual team setting are inescapable as in a collective setting.

- **Rotational Leadership**. Most members of high-performing teams are capable of leading themselves and the team, but unfortunately, they don't often get an opportunity to. Rotational leadership allows each team member to be the of the lead the team; it could be simple activities as heading up the weekly phone call, formulating agenda for the next meeting or organizing a team building activity.

- **Show Appreciation.** Make each individual feel they are valuable to the team. Although you may not be able to take everyone out to lunch, leaders can show appreciation and make employees understand how important they are to the overall success of the company. Whether it's sending gift cards and 'Thank Yous' in the emails; making simple phone calls, or doing a virtual happy hour event with your team once a month or so, can make your employees feel valued. Employees who feel valued are employees who perform better. A team culture of recognition and reward will create a great environment for collaboration, as well as engagement.

- **Virtual Team Bonding.** Research shows that the virtual teams who have participated in virtual team building exercises score significantly higher in leadership, decision making and team performance than teams who haven't. Encourage members to engage in structured team building activities as online games to bring out their competitive spirit. Playing together will develop rapport. This could be useful to acclimate the team to company policies or just to have fun. The objective of virtual team building activities and games is to help build trust among your team members, increase the level of cohesion and familiarity among your employees and to learn more about team members on a personal and professional level.

➢ **Measure Effectiveness of your team**. According to a survey conducted by FlexJobs and WorldatWork, over 80 percent of American organizations have implemented some type of flexible work arrangement. Surprisingly, though, only three percent of those same companies were measuring whether flextime actually makes people more productive and more likely to positively contribute to the bottom line. In an article for WorkFlexibility.org, Greg Kratz cited recent statistics compiled by Global Workplace Analytics that focus on large corporations. At JD Edwards telecommuters were 20 percent more productive than in-office colleagues while AT&T teleworkers worked five more hours at home than office workers. And work-from-home American Express employees were 43 percent more productive than in-office ones. If you measure productivity, you can ascertain what areas you need to improvement on to facilitate productive teamwork.

> **Get people together**. We are social beings; we were created for community, for friendship. People sharing common goals, and a common purpose—but most of all, people who care about each other and who are dedicated to helping each other. That's what teamwork should be about. We have an innate ability to connect with others. As we grow and develop we desire human interaction. Harmonious relationships do not happen by accident. We must be intentional about building relationships. Leaders need to constantly motivate remote team members to deliver their best. However, e-mails and conference calls may not be enough to keep momentum. In the absence of face to face interaction and body language, conflict often arises, and members begin to feel detached. So it's important to meet up. Get your people together to celebrate the achievement of short-term goals or to brainstorm difficult problems. Ritesh Idnani, founder and CEO of Seamless Health, a healthcare start-up that relies on dispersed teams of managers, is adamant about bringing everyone together in person at least quarterly.

Not all organizational challenges require a team; some are better handled by individuals. A team is suitable when numerous skills and viewpoints are required to accomplish a task. Team building takes a lot of care, attention and development, notwithstanding, with the proper approach you can achieve great feats. Effective teamwork lies at the heart of success for any organization. High performing teams whose members enjoy working together, doesn't happen by coincidence. Successful teams are unified because team members are supportive and put the best interests of the team foremost. They share common goals as well as the resources to achieve objectives. They are cohesive, not because team members never disagree, but because they have developed ways to quickly resolve conflicts as they occur. They are proficient because tasks are assigned based on each member's skills and interests. Therefore, ensuring the right mix of individuals is brought together can increase the probability of success. Put these tips into practice, and you'll find that your team is generating synergy and producing the results you want.

CHAPTER THREE

WHAT YOU NEED TO DO
TO BETTER ENGAGE YOUR TEAM

More than 15 years ago, Gallup Inc. pioneered employee engagement research. Gallup and other companies such as Deloitte and McKinsey, highlight the value high employee engagement generates as greater innovation, faster growth and higher customer satisfaction, to name a few. Although much is written about employee engagement, there is still a high level of and disengagement in organizations. If you ask any employee if they feel "engaged", most will tell you "not really." If you ask executives about the effectiveness of their employee engagement programmes, most likely they will tell you, "We're doing great!" Each year Gallup conducts an employee engagement poll. Their results for the first six months of 2016 showed, 32.6% of U.S. workers were engaged with their job. The actively disengaged employees cost companies $450-to-$550 billion in lost productivity each year. In summary, 6-7 out of 10 workers are turning up to work, fixing a smile on their face, and putting in the allotted hours, hoping to make it through the day with as little effort as possible. Presence does not equal performance. Non-engaged employees may just turn up at work and go through the motions. This can lead to increased absenteeism and decreased productivity. Multiple short-term periods of individual staff absence are far more injurious to productivity than single or longer-term periods where proper planning of workload redistribution can be carried out. Unscheduled absenteeism can be a real problem as well as a drain on resources, so it is imperative that all companies have procedures for addressing this. A recent Dale Carnegie research shows with increased employee engagement leads to increased employee retention due to the fact that engaged employees are less likely to leave which can dramatically impact industries with high employee turnover.

An employee who comes in early and leaves late is not necessarily an indication of an engaged employee. We must not confuse hard work with engagement and don't be deceived into thinking that more hours = improved productivity. In fact, most employees working greater than 40 hours experience a decline in productivity. Why? -

Parkinson's Law! Parkinson's Law is the adage that "work expands so as to fill the time available for its completion. People anticipate the extra hours, so they spread out their activities to fit in the time they have available. Procrastination becomes widespread, and a new mind-set is adopted; "I'm working late, so I'll do it later." The more that a company focuses on the number of hours worked, rather than the actual work accomplished, the more likely employees will alter their pace to fit the hours available. Need proof, just try telling employees that they can leave work today, whenever they finish the daily work assignments. Additionally, worker productivity is not to be confused with overall productivity. Developments in technology over the past 25 years have enabled businesses to ride a wave of productivity that has nothing to do with individual output. Companies have seen improvements in productivity, but many reasons for this, point to that of technology. Studies indicate that without the technology advancements, the accurate worker productivity statistics, adjusted for hours worked, is at the lowest point in history. Companies with engaged employees outperform the competition by as much as 202% (Gallup). The truly competitive companies of the future must attack this head on and drive the unproductive behaviours out of their organization. They must embrace a new culture where employee satisfaction and engagement is at the forefront of their business plans and objectives.

The Difference between Employee Satisfaction and Employee Engagement

Twenty years ago, more than 80% of employees were satisfied with their jobs; today only less than 50% are. The growing lack of employee satisfaction will impact on knowledge transfer and mentoring of the next generations of employees. According to Judge & Church, 2000, Job satisfaction is the most widely researched job attitude and among the most extensively researched subjects in Industrial/Organizational Psychology. Several work motivation theories have corroborated the implied role of job satisfaction. An employee can be engaged even without being satisfied with their working conditions, and vice versa. Absenteeism, tardiness, workplace conflict and insubordination are often signals of reduced job satisfaction. Satisfaction seldom leads to engagement, but engagement often leads to satisfaction. Engagement relates to how committed employees are towards achieving the company's objectives. Employee satisfaction does not "drive" enterprise value. Satisfied employees are contented with their positions — they aren't unhappy with their jobs and aren't pursuing new jobs. If you provide a competitive salary and benefits, most likely I'll be a satisfied employee. However, if you provide challenging and meaningful work, help me grow professionally, give me input into decisions while respecting me as a team member. Most likely I will be an engaged employee.

In an interesting case, consider one of the world's leading insurance company that realized employee satisfaction was actually *too high*. While its operating margin had decreased significantly, employee satisfaction had increased to record levels. After some in-depth diagnostic work, the organization found that employee satisfaction was too high among lower-performers (with too many of these) and too low among high-performers (with too few of these). To boost the culture and improve results, it began a journey to strengthen its performance orientation through greater accountability. It increased engagement and improved retention of needed talent through a refreshed value proposition. The primary goal was to increase employee productivity for the long-term, with the understanding that, in the short-term, employee satisfaction would go down.

There are three proven and fundamental drivers of sustained competitiveness and value creation: innovation, capital investment, and labour productivity. While the many indicators offered by the

Great Place to Work Institute such as camaraderie, respect, and trust are noteworthy and related to satisfaction to varying degrees, none of them matters very much if they do not translate into productivity. Companies that achieve better than average results *may* have better employee satisfaction, but more fundamentally, they have the most productive people.

> "Engagement's a big ship that won't move quickly if all we do is measure it." —Jim Harter

The truth is:

1 We aren't actively trying to inspire employees in their daily work activities even though we proclaim that we do.

2 We don't really know what employees value or how they want to work. We sit in our ivory towers and come up all these great ideas then implement changes and expect employees to be happy about it.

3 We force employees through systems, processes, and exercises to maintain control.

Employee engagement is the lifeblood of an organization. Smart leaders know they cannot succeed on their own. They surround themselves with great talented people. Raising employee engagement has become one of the highest priorities for businesses. People are spending an average eight hours a day, five days a week for about 48 weeks a year. That is a long time, and it essentially means that people are spending probably the majority of their lives at work. People are the most valuable resource of an organization, estimating almost 90% of business operating costs, so even a 5%

increase in productivity can have a significant impact on the bottom line and competitiveness of any business. Happy employees go over and beyond their responsibilities for the benefit of the company because they have that sense of belonging and ownership that drives them to work towards a common goal. In a 2014 Deloitte Global Human Capital Trends study, 78% of business leaders rate retention and engagement urgent or important. Companies are realizing that an engaged employee is a productive employee.

So how do you know an employee is engaged? An engaged employee is enthusiastic about his/her job, and voluntarily gives the organization and the customers their best. Engagement means having a genuine interest in the company. They believe in the vision and care for the company and its customers. Employee engagement is the result of a mutually beneficial relationship between employer and employee. Engaged employees create more shareholder value. If people love their work and the environment in which they work in, they will treat customers better and make fewer mistakes. An engaged employee is proud of the company they work for and will go above and beyond their call of duty to see the business succeed. They are focused on achieving objectives to meet and exceed expectations. Engaged employees are emotionally connected to the company. Glassdoor, a company that allows employees to rate their employers, reports that only 54 percent of employees recommend their employer as a place to work.

Today there are hundreds of different survey providers and benchmarking tools to help your company assess your employee's level of engagement. Employee surveys should form the foundation of any employee engagement initiative. However, there is an apparent frustration that the Employee Opinion Surveys is all too often seen as an end in itself. You must only ask for feedback if you are prepared to act upon the responses. Another concern is the reliability of the data; we all know the employees who distrust the confidentiality of the

Employee Opinion Surveys, despite the employer's assurances don't put their true feelings. If it's absolutely confidential, then managers shouldn't be trying to find out who said what. If only organizations would present such initiatives with the full intent of walking the talk. Too often these surveys are rolled out with the expectation that employees will provide verification that all is right with the company. I have even witnessed leaders trying to determine which employee voiced critical comments on a so-called anonymous survey for the sole purpose to discredit the negative feedback. If you want honest feedback, you need to ensure total confidentiality to respondents. Give employees a forum to provide anonymous feedback. For many companies, employee engagement is a score card that management uses to measure performance. Scores rise, and management seeks to compliment itself for a job well done. Companies that understand this topic go beyond engagement surveys: change the work environment, increase benefits, re-design jobs, and continuously train and develop their people. They are "mission-driven. It's time to make employee engagement a business goal. The days of the annual engagement surveys are gradually coming to an end, to be replaced by a much more integrated, holistic and real-time system that will measure and drive high levels of employee engagement.

Most employee engagement efforts are co-dependent. Engagement is almost entirely on the shoulders of the employer. Employees are always looking to management to keep them motivated. If managers pull back on the acceleration even slightly, engagement falls. Sustainable employee engagement requires that both the employee and employer contribute to its success. It occurs when the employer creates the culture and employees contribute to it because they are self-motivated.

According to Gallup if you want to measure the core elements needed to attract, focus, and keep your most talented employees. It's as simple as asking yourself questions like:

> ➤ Do my employees know what is expected of them?

> ➤ Do my employees have the materials, tools, and equipment they need to do their work right?

> ➤ Do my employees have the opportunity to do what they do best every day?

> ➤ In the past seven days, have my top performers received recognition or praise for doing good work?

> ➤ Do immediate managers, supervisors, or others at work seem to care about them as people?

Gallup has been using these questions for more than 30 years as part of its rigorous employee engagement research.

It all comes down to what do people really want?

If you ask your team the above question. The first response most people make is "money!" Yet money doesn't buy you happiness. Research shows that in North America earning over $ 75,000 a year does not increase levels of happiness. Money can make one satisfied in the short term but not fully engaged. Engagement comes from intrinsic rewards. Most studies show that it is an important factor in employee satisfaction. Research by Aon Hewitt indicates that compensation ranks among the top five drivers (but is not number one). In most cases, if compensation is not high enough, people will leave—but increasing compensation does not directly increase engagement (with certain exceptions).

HOW TO ENGAGE YOUR TEAM

The first thing you need to do is measure the existing engagement level of the organization. Knowing where the company is and what drives engagement in is key to moving forward successfully. This can be done via structured anonymous surveys. Engagement drivers differ from culture to culture and even from company to company but some aspects remain fundamental. Leaders should lead from the middle rather than the top so they could have a peripheral view of operations and be close to their team. They must be a role model. Engagement starts with you. Therefore we must recruit and train people who embody our corporate values of excellence, integrity, collaboration; who are focused on achieving our company mission; and know how to work well with others to achieve a common goal.

1 **Purpose.** Vision — Do you sell something that excites your team, and solves real problems? "The Greatness Report" recently published by Achievers found that 61 percent of employees do not know their company's cultural values and 57 percent are not motivated by their company's mission. Without purpose, there's no foundation for employee engagement. Employees who do not believe that their efforts are valued by the company have the lowest engagement levels. Create a culture where employees feel appreciated, where there is a common purpose and employees are highly involved. Show employees how their work fits into the big picture. Managers need to sit with each reporting employee and discuss the significance of the employee's job and the important deliverables to the overall strategy of the business. Employee engagement agendas should focus on helping employees believe their work matters. As Joey Reiman discusses in "The Story of Purpose," people are not motivated by the bottom line; they want to feel like they're a part of something bigger than themselves. This can be achieved by creating a sense of equality between

staff and senior management. Have a system that facilitates open door policy and transparent communication. Some organizations have complex structures, and the distinction between employees and management is alarming. Communication from executive leadership needs to be frequent and reassuring. Communicate and engage employees with a clear vision and agenda. All too often, managers cannot understand why processes are not moving quickly enough however, if people are unable to clearly envision the desired end state, there may not be a sense of urgency.

Businesses should also focus on how their products help customers and how employees' role helps the customer. Additionally, to make them feel they are making a valuable contribution get your people involved in social responsibility. When team spirit and morale is high, employee engagement will follow. Let them work together for the common good. Conduct a survey and come up with the top areas employees would like to contribute to then let them devise a plan on how we could contribute our time to bring awareness to these causes. In my previous company community-based social action programmes and environmental concerns were high on the agenda.

2 | Setting clear goals - Clear targets should be set and communicated to ensure that there are no misunderstandings on the expected deliverables. Progress is a positive force motivating employees to do their best. Management must take this into consideration when setting goals. Goals should be achievable and also should be broken down so employees can see real progress. If you give employees targets that are unrealistic, it will eventually break their spirit as their efforts can seem futile. It's like chasing a target that keeps moving that you can never reach. According to a Harvard Business study "On progress days, people were more intrinsically motivated—by interest in and enjoyment of the work itself. On setback days, they were not only less intrinsically

motivated but also less extrinsically motivated by recognition. Apparently, setbacks can lead a person to feel generally apathetic and disinclined to do the work at all...Even ordinary, incremental progress can increase people's engagement in the work and their happiness during the workday." The basic premise is that it's important to employees to achieve some sort of progress every day. Everyone wants to feel a sense of accomplishment and satisfaction in their efforts at the end of the day - that they are getting somewhere. Just minor steps forward can boost employee's engagement levels. It's gratifying for employees when they can chip away at a goal. If they can see the finish line in sight even it's far off in the distance; it will re-energize them to run harder; to give more. As Teresa Amabile, Professor at Harvard Business School stated, "Of all the things that can boost emotions, motivation, and perceptions during a workday, the single most important is making progress in meaningful work."

3 | **Give employees opportunities to use their skills and abilities.** Capitalizing on people's passions and strengths drives productivity. People work harder when they're doing the things they enjoy, especially when accomplishments fill a personal needs as well as a professional one. When employees use their significant skills on the job, they feel a sense of accomplishment and pride. They feel confident in their abilities. They will give more in comparison to someone who isn't performing in an area they are not capable in. No one wants to be uninterested and unchallenged by their work. If you have an employee, who acts as if they are bored, you need to help them find their passion. Employees want to enjoy their job. They spend more than a third of their days working, getting ready for work, and in commute to and from their place of employment. Work closely with employees who directly report to you to ensure that they are engaged, excited, and challenged to contribute and perform. Otherwise, you will lose them to a competitor who will.

4 **Granting Autonomy** - In the 1970s two psychologists, Edward Deci and Richard Ryan developed the "The Theory of Self Determination" which proposes that human beings have three intrinsic, innate psychological (motivational) drivers. This theory focuses primarily on internal sources of motivation such as a need to gain knowledge or independence, which is known as intrinsic motivation. According to this theory, people are intrinsically motivated, and become self-determined, when they experience a high degree of competence, connection and autonomy. When any of these three motivational drivers were not engaged, the internal motivation decreased. Autonomy was included as one of the factors. Human beings want to be in control; they want to have choices. Employees want meaningful work, and they want flexibility in how, when and where they work. If an employee can't see a path to continued growth in their current organization, they are likely to look elsewhere for such opportunity. Give people responsibility and challenges that will help them to grow. Let them come up with ideas. When employees have a choice or say in the operations, they become far more engaged in the outcomes. When people own their choices, better outcomes are the result. Don't just tell them what to do. I have found that empowered team members are not only more satisfied but are far more willing to execute an order even when it is commanded. In my early career, I worked for a company that employed scientific management to boost productivity. There was no real leadership (vision and inspiration) only management (command and control). The culture was basically do as you are told. Suggestions and recommendations by employees or even results of viewpoint surveys were ignored. Management didn't accept the results. Their analysis of results centred on whether employees understood the questions. Poorly performing managers were not even recommended for remedial training. It was just, "well next year we know we will improve." Employees became disengaged and focused solely

on their salary. That was their only high point. Most individuals did nothing extra outside of their job specifications. At 4:00 pm on the dot, employees could be seen leaving the office, as if there was a fire drill taking place. Team spirit and morale was extremely low. I felt stifled. Thus, I didn't stay there very long. Many individuals wanted to leave but because of debts or accumulated retirement earnings remained. In cases like this, a company can form an Employee Action Team who works with management to evaluate the results of employee surveys and put measures in place to increase employee engagement.

5 | **Training and Development** - Is your business committed to employee development? How do your leaders demonstrate it? Do employees see and feel leaders' commitment? Leaders set the tone and model the organization's commitment to developing employees' capabilities. The best development is planned around the long-standing 70-20-10 learning framework. These percentages are just guidelines, not inflexible rules that have to be followed each and every time. This model says that about 70% of development comes from on-the-job experience, 20% comes from feedback and examples, and 10% comes from courses and reading. The model has been a point of discussion for nearly 20 years, yet most companies are still focused on that 10%, or formal learning. A survey, from the American Psychological Association, found that 41 percent of workers said they are stressed or tense at work, due to having too much work, long hours, low salaries or a sense that there is no room for professional growth. Many traditional managers still believe that only money and status motivates people. But research shows the opposite. One such study was carried out by *Development Dimensions International* and published in the UK Times newspaper. They interviewed more than 1,000 employees from organizations employing more than 500 workers, and found many to be lacking commitment, bored, and looking for a new

job. Salary actually came fifth in the reasons individuals gave for leaving their jobs. The main reasons were a lack of stimulus and limited opportunities for advancement. Most people cherish some form of ambition and want to move forward. The important role of the organization is to link that ambition to facilitate the individual›s growth. When employees have access to opportunities, this will enable them to be satisfied, leading them to become an asset to the organisation and inspiring others along the way.

Employee engagement soars when it's a priority and looked upon with purpose and intention. When people feel they are moving forward, adding to their skill base, learning new concepts, and stretching their capabilities, motivation tends to remain high. Personal growth enhances self-esteem and self-worth. The worst place an employee can be, is stuck in an organization where there are no opportunities for growth and advancement. It feels like being trapped in a box. For highly-driven and ambitious individuals, it can be likened to putting an eagle in a chicken coop and clipping their wings. Leaders need to know their employees and what motivates them. Be fair and transparent with filling internal job vacancies. Employee loyalty is a thing of the past. Who really thinks of starting off their career and remaining with the same company until they retire anymore? The demographics of the workforce has changed considerably, and people are no longer settling for just a basic salary. People are operating more like free agents. They want more. They are actively seeking new challenges. If you are heading a small business and job openings are few and far in between; Make cross training, job rotation and mentoring available and gave employees more responsibility. Assign challenging projects that motivate employees and gave them stretch targets which will cause them to grow. If they have plateaued and there is nothing else to look forward to, they will become disengaged. Another issue I have noticed becoming prominent is new employees training schedule is curtailed to expedite the transition process. What happens is you have speedily moved them to level five when they have only finished level three. These 'newbies' are then thrown out into the ocean and expected to swim with the sharks. The effects for someone who isn't a quick learner is long lasting. They are unsure and keep asking questions and making mistakes. This results in high turnover and disengagement. Adequate training should be provided for new employees as well as those who are already in the system that have assumed a new role.

6 | **Focus on Relationship Building.** Get to know your employees. Let them feel a part of the team and a part of something much greater. TinyPulse research found that peers have much greater impact on engagement. People want to work with great people and have fun at work. Be present and engaged with your team. Be a good listener. When you are speaking with an employee, don't seem distracted or that you are not listening, make them feel they are the only person in the room. Be interested in their personals lives and their goals and aspirations. Spending time together -

not working - is one of the simplest ways to build relationships within your team. Encourage your team to sit together at lunch. Have in-house relationship building activities like karaoke and food and designing your work space competitions. Include offsite activities as well. Sometimes a change in environment does well for everyone. Team building activities strengthen the relationships that are working and help to repair ones that are weak. Research has indicated an employee is happy at their job when they have a best friend at work. The co-workers with whom he/she sits, interacts, and serves with on teams, are important components of an employee's work environment. **Socializin**g is a key element of engagement. It gives people a boost in mood. When your team knows one another, they'll be more comfortable collaborating and sharing ideas which leads to faster, better outcomes. Employers can encourage office celebrations for holidays and birthdays. These do not need to be expensive. Socializing is not limited to office hours. Encourage out of office get-togethers such as volunteering for a good cause. This gives employees the opportunity to develop relationships outside of the workplace while promoting the company in a positive way. Community service is a great way to build a great reputation, and it is a happiness booster for employees. Make it a team sport. Get everyone to participate, and set the example by making time to do so yourself.

7 **Show employees that you truly care about them**. Does your company appreciate employees, treat them with respect, and provide compensation and benefits that demonstrate this respect and appreciation? Are you actually building and nurturing an organization where employees feel listened to, valued and cared about? For some employees, the workload is too high, and pressure is constant. Divide the workload: When you work in teams, the workload is distributed among the team members resulting in reduced stress. Show them you care about them as a

70

human being and not just consider them a robot on your cog-like production line. Start small and see where it goes. Recognize the value of a workers personal lives. Everyone has personal obligations; we're not machines that have the ability to turn on and off everything else in our life just because we come to work. In reality, when employees talk about dissatisfaction with their work, many times it contains very personal stories of how the company or management was not sensitive to their personal responsibilities. Promote work-life balance. When employees realize that you don't care about them by infringing on their personal time, everything you do regarding relationship building activities will seem superficial. There will be a lack of buy-in. If you support their work-life balance, then they will support your vision with everything they have. According to a March 2015 survey by Totaljobs, a U.K.-based job placement agency: "Work-life balance is by far a universal concern for 50% of the workforce." *Take a sincere interest in your people and provide them with the right tools they need to carry out their job functions.*

8 | **Refuse to allow favouritism or unfair management practices** – Favouritism comes in many different forms like recognizing or communicating with specific persons more than others. Unfair practices relate to how vacancies are filled, disciplining inconsistently and even in how a leader allows leeway in work schedules. This fosters poor team spirit and in some cases a drop in productivity. Managers also lose credibility when they refuse to hold themselves accountable and palm of the blame on others. The core function of managers is to: inform, educate, motivate, clarify, seek feedback and act on that feedback. When you accept feedback and accountability, you are putting your team before yourself, and you come across as authentic.

In 2013, Jim Clifton, Chairman of the Gallup Organization, wrote:

"The single biggest decision your company makes every day is who you name manager. This is the conclusion Gallup draws from decades of data and interviews with 25 million employees…. but companies keep getting this decision wrong, over and over again. In fact, the people picked to be managers account for the majority of variance in almost all performance-related outcomes. Yet leaders will spend hundreds of billions of dollars every year on everything but hiring the right managers. They'll buy miserable employees latte machines for their offices, give them free lunch and sodas, or even worse -- just let them all work at home, hailing an "enlightened" policy of telecommuting. Some of these practices might even earn your company a business magazine's Great Place to Work award. The problem is, employee engagement in America isn't budging. Of the country's roughly 100 million full-time employees, an alarming 70 million (70%) are either not engaged at work or are actively disengaged. That number has remained stagnant since Gallup began tracking the U.S. working population's engagement levels in 2000."

Poor leadership costs UK £6 billion a year. According to Ros Taylor Research, 77% of staff say their boss is not interested in their growth and development. 90% say their boss ignores poor performers. 79% claim their boss sets unclear objectives and 89% say their boss is unreceptive to new ideas. A Harvard Business Review study states that when employees report feeling respected by their bosses, 89% say they felt greater job satisfaction, 55% report feeling more engaged, and 92% say it was easier to focus at work. Employees don't need to be friends with their manager, but they need to have a working relationship. The manager is a big part of their daily lives at work to have a strained relationship. The manager interacts with the employee to provide direction and feedback and connects the employee to the larger organization. To have a toxic relationship with the supervisor an employee reports to demoralises the employee's engagement, commitment and confidence.

Since managers have the most contact with their team, they have the power to inspire them to give their best. There is no greater feeling than knowing your manager has your back. The worst is working in an environment where it is evident your manager dislikes you. Remember the employee is the number one customer. A good connection between a manager and an employee builds a great foundation for employee engagement. It's just disturbing to see that in some companies, management has no clue about their employees' personal or family life. They are solely fixated on their professional contribution. Employees want to work with managers who will help them grow their skills and inspire them to do great work. Studies show, if a manager ignores an employee, there is a 40% chance that they will be actively disengaged. If the manager is at least paying attention to them - even if they are focusing on weaknesses - the chance of being actively disengaged drops to 22%. Whereas if a manager is primarily focusing on one's strengths, the chance of an employee being actively disengaged drops to just 1%.

The absence of a sufficient level of true leadership, throughout the world, is causing widespread organizational stagnation. Too many people in leadership roles are more concerned with protecting their own self-interest than; creating a future vision, inspiring support from their followers and improving the lives of others. There must be a culture of trust; managers have to trust employees to meet their business targets and cooperate to get the job done. On the other hand, employees must trust their manager to provide them with the right inputs to get the job done.

9 **Encourage and motivate your employees.** I always tell my employees "I believe in you; I know you can do it." Your confidence in your teams' abilities will energize them and cause a surge in their commitment and productivity. There is nothing like having someone believe in you. I remember sharing a leadership article with my team. One of my employees Susanna afterwards said she enjoyed the article, but it was not for her as she is not a leader. I pulled her up at once and let her know the traits she possessed as taking the initiative, seeing projects through and setting the right example showed leadership. Later on, that day as Susanna passed by my office; I could see her whole countenance and body language had changed. Show your team that you believe in them by emotionally supporting them, and they will want to exceed your expectations. Susanna went from an average performer to a top performer. Never underestimate the impact that positive words can have on your team.

10 **Embracing Diversity** – Diversity is essential in successful groups. Diversity of ideas and backgrounds builds a more creative, adaptive and innovative workplace. The point of teamwork should be to bring together people who think differently and bring a range of views. Understandably, the role of the leader is to utilize diversity and to be able to propose specific solutions that others in the group agree with. When we talk about embracing diversity, this includes; multiple perspectives, ways of being, and communication styles. For example, being bold in one culture is accepted and appropriate, but in another, it is unacceptable and inappropriate. Furthermore, developing team norms within purposeful communities is imperative in creating an actual environment where various viewpoints are valued. Finally, creating a culture of collaboration and learning cultural differences and ways of communicating, will help with respectful dialogue and mindful ways of disagreeing. Research has proven that companies who disregard diversity as an important component in their business strategy have a higher percentage of disengaged workers while organisations that seek to embrace employee diversity and inclusion have higher levels of employee engagement and are better positioned to obtain the well-known benefits of a high engagement as increased employee performance. Employees with the highest level of engagement perform 20 percent better and are 87 percent less likely to leave the organization, according to a survey by TowersPerrin. A study by the Hay Group also found engaged employees were as much as 43% more productive. Lorna Donatone, Region Chair for North America and CEO of Schools Worldwide stated, "For 50 years, Sodexo has been a people-centred organization. Our employees provide quality of life services to 75 million consumers around the world. That's why diversity and inclusion is at the heart of our business strategy and our brand promise. Our inclusive work culture allows us to respect and understand the diverse markets where we do business. It also enriches our

workplace by improving quality of life for our employees, which gives us a real competitive advantage." A culture that values diversity will try to ensure that everyone feels comfortable and respected at work. Bringing people with different backgrounds and perspectives together will contribute to your organization's long-term success. Don't just tolerate diversity, celebrate it.

11 **Encourage honest feedback and take action.** In this environment for employee satisfaction and retention to thrive, it is of vital importance to know which factors most affect employee satisfaction. One of the secrets of successful corporation lays in open and respectful working atmosphere. Communication both up and down the chain is essential. A company who suppresses employee's voices, cannot grow beyond a certain point because it doesn't know what its weak points and necessary areas of improvement are. Every company needs to grant employees the freedom to "speak up." Listen and learn, not only from top to bottom but also from the bottom to the top and to each other. Sadly, most people in positions of authority put their own personal gain ahead of everyone else's. Until that changes, they may listen, but they won't necessarily hear what is being said, act on it, and give credit to others. As a leader, I have no problem with people disagreeing with me and encourage them to speak up. You lose your effectiveness if your team just sits back and lets you make all the decisions. If you see a better way to do something I am all ears. Too often I find that the indication of free speech tolerance is a mechanism used to indict those that do not agree with the masses. I've seen the person who speaks out get singled out. I've also seen other team members who encourage others into thinking they should speak up for the sake of the team, lurk back into the shadows when the victimization begins. Some of us have had the experience of working at companies where you raise an important issue to management, and nothing ever gets done about it. That sort of outright

indifference and inaction can have a negative effect on employee morale. On the other hand, when you make attempts to address employees' concerns, their commitment to, and confidence in the organization can skyrocket. If you listen and acknowledge that shows people, you value their opinion, so they will continue to give it. Companies should make a stronger effort to listen to employee concerns, work towards a solution then follow up. Sometimes, problems cannot be fixed for a variety of reasons (insufficient funding, lack of resources, etc.). However, that does not excuse the employer from at least trying to find a solution and getting back to the person/people who raised that concern. It's surprising what even a simple email or quick conversation to address what has been done to improve existing conditions will do for employee morale. Just knowing that your input has been taken seriously as an employee is motivating.

12 **Establish consistent performance review cycles and Reward and Recognize.** Employees need to understand and be clear about their job functions? Employee reviews are a central component of a productive company. All too frequently, employees get comfortable in what they are doing, and without consistent feedback, they will fall into a routine. **Do you regularly coach** employees in the spirit of showing them how to get work done? Leaders need to take the time to meet with their employees, develop goals and objectives and follow up on progress. How many employees in your company spend time on things with no increase in productivity?

Additionally, recognize and reward employees for recommended behaviours. Reward and recognition is an important part of employee empowerment. When employees feel under-compensated, unnoticed and unappreciated, don't expect engagement. The basic needs of employees must be met for employees to give that extra effort in work. For successful employee engagement, recognition plays a significant role. Regardless of the size of the success, recognition has to be meaningful and memorable. Recognition highlights that you value employee's contribution and encourages them to keep working diligently. It rewards positive behaviour and drives every employee to perform at their best. According to surveys managers are generally quick to call out employees when performance is poor or when goals are not being achieved. Rather than complain about the numbers not being right and focusing on what people are doing wrong, instead highlight achievements in spite of how small it may be. Small progress is still progress. Compliment them on their work in meetings and emails (carbon copy the whole office). Show impartiality. Remind all team members of their importance and don't limit the success to only one department. One of the biggest flaws in the annual performance review is that it only centres on major achievements - completing a major project, closing a big deal, etc. Those victories tend to be few and far between. Big victories are definitely worth celebrating, but recognizing little victories is also important. Celebrating can be as simple as calling out an accomplishment in a weekly meeting and clapping for the person or team that accomplished their goal, or it can mean taking the team offsite for lunch or dessert. In our monthly reward and recognition programme, we recognise top performers as well as those who are improving. We also reward everyone with tokens so no one is left out and they know their contribution is valued. We focus heavily on recognizing and rewarding team performance trying to reduce the emphasis on individual performance. Teamwork is at the core of sustainable success. I use "Thank you for... and I appreciate you for..." very often, Feedback is great when it is timely, specific and actionable. Give out thank yous as prompt as possible after an event, behaviour or result, and let employees know how it supports the overall organizational strategy. Be sure to say "thank you *for* [fill it in with the specific behaviour or result that matters]. An effective approach is to reward employees with something that would be meaningful to them. Additionally, create moments that an employee will remember and tie back to a particular accomplishment at their company. For example, if an employee is recognized for their hard work with a gift voucher for a massage or a meal at a fine restaurant, that memory will remain with them. Therefore, every time they recall that experience, they will remember feeling valued and be inspired to continue performing at a higher level.

13 **Promote Health and Well Being.** Even though the United States enjoys one of the highest standards of living in the world; Americans need more doctors, take more medications,

and experience more heart disease and cancer than nearly any undeveloped country. Poor health is not only personally damaging to employees; it is detrimental to business. Promote healthy living. Encourage your team to eat healthy, drink sufficient water and get adequate rest. A healthy body leads to a healthier mind which leads to less stress, and the acute thinking ability needed in the workplace. You can implement practical mind-body-spirit health initiatives that help improve attention, promote mindfulness, reduce stress, eliminate bad habits, and increase overall energy levels. Create healthy competitions: An office challenge that encourages each person to reach a goal within a specific period can be motivating and fun. A contest to complete a certain amount of steps each day is a great way to get employees moving and can increase fitness levels. Create team effort: Doing a fitness based team building programme can go a long way to building a cohesive group, plus it gets everyone out of the office.

14 **Invest in lower turnover** – HR expert Dr. John Sullivan once wrote: Asking employees at time of termination "why are you leaving" is like asking your spouse "how to improve the marriage" on the day before the divorce is final. By that time it's too late. Don't wait until it's too late. It is important to know which factors most affect employee satisfaction. A survey, by the *Society for Human Resource Management* (SHRM) looked at 24 factors that are regularly thought to relate to employee satisfaction. The study found that employees identified job security, benefits (especially health care) with the importance of retirement benefits, compensation/pay, opportunities to use skills and abilities, and feeling safe in the work environment rising with the age of the employee. Many studies have been conducted on the impact of turnover in organizations, and they all arrive at the same conclusion, high turnover is costly to a business, and they pay for it dearly in productivity. Training new employees to be as efficient

as current staff is only part of the equation. There is also lost productivity in training the new team member. When turnover is so high that people recognize it as an issue, the remaining employees will begin to look outside the company for other opportunities. They start to question their own decision to stay when they see people looking happy going elsewhere. Moreover, teamwork suffers greatly because solid, long-term relationships are fundamental to teamwork, and those relationships can't grow in a company with a revolving door.

15 **Balance Work with Play** – People are not androids. We have emotions. We spend more than half of the time of day when we are not sleeping at the office. If this place is not inspiring for you or if every day you do not look forward to being there then is it really worth it? Some people seem to forget the idea that "All work and No Play makes Jack a Dull Boy." Yes, employees already know that they come to the office to do a job, but you should not stop them from having fun as well. There have been many studies that substantiate that people perform best at tasks that they enjoy or if the environment in which they are working is an enjoyable one. Socializing may seem like an unnecessary approach, but having a team that gets along well is an essential part of making a more productive workplace. When your team feels a connection to each other, they are more likely not to want to let each other down.

New Tools and Approaches

While the engagement survey is still used in many companies, new tools and techniques have been developed that measure happiness, alignment, and job satisfaction in real time. These tools include analytics applications and rapid pulse surveys that correlate retention and performance to job factors and day to day tools that allow employees to honestly express their feelings.

Gartner, a world-leading information technology research and advisory company, had predicted that by 2015, 40% of Global 1000 organizations would adopt gamification as the primary mechanism to transform business operations. Gamification is the new game changer for employee engagement and is the trending business buzzword. It enables companies to take standard parts of the work day and make them more engaging and enjoyable for employees. Through IT technology, games are developed that centre on everyday tasks and responsibilities which are incorporated in employee training and recruiting. This, in turn, results in a win-win situation with improved quality and productivity.

In their Gamification 2020 report, Gartner predicts that gamification in combination with other technology trends such as analytics will have a significant influence on the below aspects of an organization:

❖ Innovation

❖ The design of employee performance

❖ Globalisation of higher education

❖ Emergence of customer engagement platforms

❖ Gamification of personal development

Gamification has helped organizations to establish and manage tailored benchmarks; to review employee performance, improve progress and encourage learning. The cases for using gamification are numerous and rising. Through gamification, companies can strengthen employees understanding of the company goals. This, in turn, will foster a greater inclination in employees to want to contribute to the organization's objectives.

Limits of Gamification

➢ **Making incorrect assumptions about learners** - We assume that younger workers are technology-savvy and will engage in any game we create. The truth is not all millennials enjoy games, the same as not all baby boomers dislike them. Gamification is only effective when it encourages specific behaviours to achieve specific goals. It needs to account for differences in users' personalities.

➢ **Unrealistic expectations -** Gamification can be used to encourage people to work better but may not be useful for making people work harder. Additionally, don't exclude other methods of learning: Gamification won't work for everyone, not everyone has the same learning style. Gamification is promising, but it can't miraculously cure deeper organizational problems.

➢ **Poor design.** Try to keep things as simple as possible. If the design doesn't make the game work smoothly, employees can get confused or frustrated especially when they don't know their way around the learning content, and are having trouble with getting to the next level. IT needs to translate the features into a usable interface.

➢ **Lack of planning and strategy.** Many managers focus on their own goals. Crafting a gamified experience that engages employees, calls for a good understanding of employee goals. Gamification emphasizes the inherent value of an activity. If the activity has no intrinsic value to the performer, gamification is not useful.

> **Overusing rewards**. Rewards are worthwhile only if they mean something in real life. Gaining points must be linked with actual performance and growth.

Once companies treat their workers fairly within the framework of gamification, the potential for changing workplace engagement and satisfaction is boundless. "The best gamification occurs when players achieve a company's goals by pursuing their own." —Brian Burke, Gartner Institute

The Generation Gap

It's also important to understand the composition of your team. Generational gaps do exist. Studies reveal that employee engagement differences exists across generations. A Mercer's 2015 Inside Employees Minds survey revealed numbers behind the values held by multigenerational employees — **Baby Boomers** (1946 to 1964)**, Generation X** (mid-1960s to 1970s), **Generation Y/Millennials** (1980s to mid-1990s) and **Generation Z** (mid 1990s to early 2000s). While base pay is most important to all employees, younger generations ranked flexible schedule very high when compared to older generations, who are likely to have more family demands. Baby Boomers and Generation X ranked Retirement Plan and Low Heath Care costs at the top of things they valued while Generation Y and Z put Career Opportunities at the top of their list. The research also indicated that 44% of workers age 18–34 are seriously considering leaving their organization. "If employers want to remain competitive in today's market, they need to create a strategic workforce plan — one that aligns to an evolved value proposition — based on the dynamics of this rapidly changing talent landscape. The plan must consider both engaged and disengaged workers, who account for about a fifth of the overall workforce, according to our research. Perhaps more than those who leave, this group has the potential to harm morale and productivity. If your employees stay, you want them engaged and productive." —Patrick Tomlinson, North American Business Leader for Talent at Mercer

A marketing company had a high turnover rate and upon investigation, they realized 80% of their staff was comprised of employees from Generation Y and Z, yet their compensation plan and culture was tailored to suit individuals belonging to older generations. This called for a redesigning of the organizational structure and the rewards system with a greater focus on employee empowerment and growth and development opportunities. Understanding the common preferences of Generations Y and Z helped the organization to turnaround employee engagement which positively impacted employee retention. Keeping up with social change driven by younger employees can also be a pathway for keeping your organization relevant.

CONCLUSION

Employee engagement is an inside job. If your team aren't fully engaged, to find the problem; take a good hard look in the mirror. Businesses that fail to take positive steps toward improving job satisfaction and employee engagement are doomed to poor productivity and high turnover. Is your work environment conducive to employee satisfaction and engagement? Do you provide fun events, celebrations, and team building activities that make employees feel that the organization is a great place to work? Many companies implement a range of programmes to try and boost employee morale. However, giving sweet treats and increasing break times can only work for so long before the novelty fades. Many employees can feel belittled by such actions and would rather a financial reward or – a resounding demonstration of "Thank You! Sustainability is essential. Employees are sick and tired of single initiatives that die off whenever someone is too busy, or the programme is seen to be financially unpopular. Research shows that when initiatives come and go, staff is more dissatisfied and mistrusting than they were before such programmes were initiated. Evaluate your status, develop your strategy and stay with it. Monitor progress regularly and improve as needed. Employees appreciate a workplace in which there is a shared vision, management is accessible, the direction is clear, and communication is transparent. Your overall culture keeps employees – or turns them away. Programmes and processes designed to improve satisfaction and engagement must be in place and include respect, communication, recognition and appreciation of accomplishments and ongoing improvement. Once leaders begin to intentionally choose to make people their principal focus, their effectiveness rises.

Creating a high-performance work environment is a complex issue. You have to communicate the mission and vision, select and train the right people. Then you have to continuously improve and redesign the work environment to ensure it is contemporary, relevant, humane, and enjoyable. Depending on your current scores, employee engagement will take a while to increase - It is a process. Organizations need engaged employees to achieve and sustain success.

CHAPTER FOUR

CAPITALIZING ON
THE POWER OF DIVERSITY

Culture is "the set of attitudes, values, beliefs and behaviours shared by a group of people, but different for each individual, communicated from one generation to the next" (Matsumoto, 1996). Cultural diversity is a reality in the modern workplace. Diversification of the workplace is largely due to two factors: primarily the changing composition of national populations and then globalization. National populations are changing because of the combined effect of high birth rates of minority ethnic groups and increased immigration. The work landscape has changed significantly in the past 50 years. The latest census results confirm that the ethnic composition of the U.S. is changing at a rate faster than anyone has anticipated. "China is expected to surpass the US regarding nominal GDP by 2026 (in 9 years). India, the 'strongest emerging market' is expected to jump to third place with real growth averaging around 5% by 2050." (The Economist Intelligence Unit, 2015). Canada has taken the world leadership role in embracing multiculturalism and diversity. A recent article in the Economist titled "Liberty Moves North" points that while its Southern neighbour is planning to build walls to block Mexican immigrants, Canada plans to take in 300,000 immigrants in 2017 – that is 1% of its population. Globalization has meant that today every company, small, medium or large, faces increased competition both locally and internationally. Globalization has given birth to diversity in the workplace as organizations are composed of employees from different cultures and backgrounds. The world is moving into the modern age due to globalization and advent of new technology. In recent years globalization has led to more interaction amongst organizations and people from various cultural and ethnic backgrounds. Diversity and multiculturalism in the workplace differ, for the reason that multiculturalism can be viewed as a subdivision of diversity. Multiculturalism and a diversified workforce is a necessity for a company to maintain and succeed in today's society. Managing a culturally diverse workforce in today's organizations is therefore of great importance. Failure to develop a diversified workforce can hinder the abilities of a business to reach its' full potential.

Diversity started to gain popularity as a business construct in the 1980s. Diversity is synonymous with receptivity, variety, and enhanced growth. Managing diversity in organizations comes down to accepting and appreciating differences in your workforce. Diversity in the workplace can take the form of variations in age, gender, religion, disability, ethnicity, national backgrounds and culture. Diversity is basically all ways in which people differ and not just the more apparent ones of ethnicity, gender and disability. However, diversity alone is not enough. It's the inclusion factor that is crucial. Does everyone feel welcome? Can everyone speak up and be heard? Do you accept people who look differently? Having a diverse workforce can increase an organisation's productivity and efficiency. Research has shown that companies that drive innovation by leveraging the knowledge and ideas of their employees meet product revenue targets 46 % more often than industry peers. (IT Global, 2011). Cross-cultural diversity can form a source of creativity and innovation to drive competitiveness of organisations.

As humans, we view the world from a very narrow perspective: our own. Realistically, we must acknowledge the limitations of our own culture and that with every culture there lies at its foundation cultural bias. PricewaterhouseCoopers', a long recognized best place to work, stated on their company webpage, "At PwC, we believe in confronting the hard realities—and then doing something about it." There is great conflict in the world which originates from ignorance. Therefore, we need to encourage dialogue, which is a bridge on the dichotomy of acceptance. Years ago American patriot Thomas Jefferson wrote the famous words, "We hold these truths to be self-evident, that all men are created equal." However agreeable the sentiment, history shows that this view was anything but "self-evident." There can be unconscious bias as we naturally gravitate to people who look and sound like us. There is a tendency for people to be attracted to people "like themselves." Sodexo, a global leader in quality-of-life services, is well known for its openness and strength to recognize bias. The company was recognized with one of Canada's Best Diversity Employers awards for two years in a row. Barry Telford, President of Sodexo Canada stated, "Diversity is not just about each group getting their moment. We must all work together to identify bias and make a commitment at all levels of the organization not to overlook our most talented and resilient team members."

It takes time and significant effort to change as we may harbour certain beliefs and attitudes that impede the process. Ethnocentrism by definition is the evaluation of other cultures according to preconceptions originating in the standards and customs of one's own culture. This can lead to stereotyping. Stereotypes are preconceived opinions on how things or groups of people are characterized. Studies have shown that stereotyping can occur unconsciously. Stereotyping occurs between various cultural groups and therefore can obstruct an organization's efforts to include diversity through resistance. There is also the **"glass ceiling barrier".** The glass ceiling is "an invisible barrier that separate women and minorities from top management positions" They can look up through the glass ceiling and see management, but there are invisible obstacles that block their own advancement (Daft 1997). These roadblocks hinder efforts to make the most of the unique talents and abilities other groups possess. Acknowledging limitations and biases are building blocks to meaningful change. With this candidness and in our willingness to discuss where we are and what we need to do, is the catalyst to propel us forward. We all would like peace and harmony in our lives. We need to focus on these values and begin to create tangibles that support these goals.

Facebook rebuilt its unconscious bias training course and even posted it online. "At Facebook, we believe that understanding and managing unconscious bias can help us build stronger, more diverse and inclusive organizations. These videos are designed to help us recognize our biases so we can reduce their negative effects in the workplace. Surfacing and countering unconscious bias is an essential step towards becoming the people and companies we want to be." Facebook seeks to remove unconscious biases in the workforce against minorities, women and subgroups like working mothers.

Understanding that cultural differences exist and the way that they impact the workforce is the key to embracing diversity in our organizations. Incorporating diversity into an organization will take considerable time. It starts with changing the mind-set of people and the organization's culture. The learnability of a practice consists of the type and amount of effort, study, accumulated comprehension, and expertise required to understand the information and know-how involved in work activities (McIver et al., 2012). Learnability captures the ease with which someone who is unfamiliar with a practice is able to develop the ability to perform the activities involved in the work process. Adoption of diversity as a business goal is not enough to receive its maximum benefits; diversity should be reflected in the organization's culture. To manage diversity effectively, there should be support and genuine commitment from all members of the organisation. Commitment must start at the top which then cascades through the entire organisation. Top level support and commitment to diversity is crucial, as well as the commitment from supervisors and managers. It would result in almost everyone getting on board. According to The DiversityInc Top 50 most diverse companies across the globe; Companies, where the CEO is actively engaged in diversity efforts, stand out. AT&T was fourth on the list in 2016. AT&T Chairman and CEO Randall Stephenson oversees the company's executive diversity council and founded it in 2008. Kaiser Permanente held the No. 1 spot as it continues its commitment to diversity and inclusion. According to the company, "Kaiser Permanente fosters a highly diverse culture as a cornerstone of its mission and business strategy." This commitment starts at the top with its Chairman and CEO Bernard J. Tyson. Tyson personally signs off on executive compensation tied to diversity, diversity goals and metrics and achievements for supplier diversity. Kaiser Permanente has also achieved high success in employing minorities at the senior level. "Competitiveness Through Management of Diversity: Effects on Stock Price Valuation," report, found that firms that received Department of Labor awards for their success in implementing voluntary action policies resulted in a boost in their share price within 10 days of the announcement.

7 STEPS TO EMBRACE DIVERSITY AND INCLUSION:

1 **Assess the Current Culture**

Firstly, knowing where you are, is the starting point. Conduct a review of the organization on the religious and cultural diversity of the organization. HR could provide these statistics. What about suppliers? Is there supplier diversity? Do you use companies owned by people from underrepresented groups? Few companies are as effective as Ford when it comes to supplier diversity. In November of 2014, The National Minority Supplier Development Council named Carla Preston of Ford Motor Company a Minority Supplier Development Leader. In 2013, Preston's efforts led to Ford including 16 new Tier 1 diverse suppliers to its network, totalling $4.8 million in spending. The same year, Ford granted $1.08 billion of new business to diverse suppliers. Once a company knows where they stand - the results are in, it's time to form strategic solutions. Diversity is a long-term goal which cannot be fixed with one simple solution. Weigh your possibilities and decide the best course of action for the company. Identify the areas where improvements are needed to ensure better cultural understanding for team effectiveness and review policies and practices to see if there are enough shared moments to learn and understand each other's culture. Events conducted by some organizations as Harmony Day are great places to start. However, organizations need to look beyond Harmony Day and work towards embracing diversity into the structure of the organization. As Race Discrimination Commissioner, Allianz CEO, Niran Peiris stated, "Australian workplaces are good at celebrating cultural diversity events in their lunch rooms, but the real issue is about achieving cultural diversity in the "corridors of power", because unless people have role models, "they won't aspire to do the things that you would expect talented people to do." It is not only about having diversity within a company but leveraging that diversity to produce better products and services.

| 2 | **Change Structures to support Diversity**

When preparing to deal with the issues surrounding cultural diversity a focal point must be the structure of the organization. What does your organization have in place for Diversity & Inclusion? Leaders should increase implementation by changing policies, structures, and systems to support diversity. These include fairness in recruitment and career advancement, as well as providing flexible benefits and programmes.

To measure Individual Recruiters' Effectiveness, here are some suggested metrics by Dr. John Sullivan, an internationally recognized HR thought-leader from the Silicon Valley:

- ➢ % of diverse candidates' resumes of all initial candidates presented to hiring managers

- ➢ % of diverse candidates interviewed by hiring managers

- ➢ % of job offers extended to diverse candidates

- ➢ % turnover rate of diversity hires within a year

> ➤ Average diverse applicants' satisfaction rate (from a survey)

> ➤ Average manager satisfaction score (from a survey) after a diversity hire

> ➤ Average on-the-job performance rating of diversity hires after one year

No matter the size or number of diverse employees in your organization, there are always more ways to improve. Analyzing your job descriptions and other recruitment practices can make a big difference in your candidate pool. If the structure of the organization is not accommodating for a multicultural workforce, your attempts to develop a more diverse workforce will crumble.

According to Victoria Lawes, Head of UK Resourcing at Deloitte, one of the biggest issues facing the UK is a lack of social mobility. Therefore individuals born into low-income families, regardless of their talent do not have the same opportunities as those born into more privileged situations. This means that students from more affluent families tend to go to top universities, which leads to them getting higher profile jobs. So, in a move to help social mobility in Britain and to ensure applicants are assessed based on their accomplishments (and not on their backgrounds), Deloitte decided to hide which university applicants went to from their Hiring Managers. "We are calling it school and university-blind interviewing," Lawes stated in an interview with LinkedIn. "What we really want to do is ensure that, whoever is recruiting isn't consciously or unconsciously favouring a person who attended a certain school or university." Their aim is that this policy will lead to a more diverse team at Deloitte - one with more "diversity of thought" and "diversity of ideas".

It's important to establish your diversity brand. If your organization already has made or is making significant diversity and inclusion progress, then prominently showcase this on your company's career page and social media channels. Some companies include a diversity clause in their office conduct guidelines for example, "we do not discriminate by race, gender, religion, beliefs and culture." Make sure this is communicated both internally and externally and followed up by action. Regulators in some European countries have already introduced diversity targets for boards, such as those set out in the UK Equality Act 2010. Most of the time, when companies focus on diversity, it generally centres on class, race or gender. This is why some companies often make progress in only one area of diversity. Often those with disabilities tend to get overlooked. Walgreens have made it their priority to hire disabled workers – which account for 10% of their employees who work in their distribution centres. And this decision has significantly paid off for Walgreens. The Walgreens Windsor, Connecticut distribution centre which has the highest percentage of disabled workers, was found to be their safest and most productive centre. Organizations, should therefore, adopt tailored programmes and make more targeted efforts within specific areas of diversity and this can be achieved by building relationships with cultural groups and organizations that work with diverse communities.

Julie Goodridge, CEO of NorthStar Asset Management, who is an outspoken advocate for corporate diversity. "I'm always looking for board diversity...How many women and people of color are running this company?" The key, Goodridge said, is to not think that having one person of color or one woman on a board is progress. The truth is, it's more likely to isolate that individual and make it difficult for them to voice opinions confidently. "Your job is twice as hard when you're isolated," she said. In the United Kingdom, a 3.5 percent increase in earnings has been observed with every 10 percent increase in gender diversity.

3 | Diversity Awareness Training and Coaching

Once the organizational structure is established in such a way that will promote the multicultural workforce, the next phase is training. According to research by the Level Playing Field Institute, more than 2 million employees a year leave their jobs solely to recurring instances of unconscious biases or unfairness. Organizations should have diversity awareness training to help people become aware of their own cultural boundaries and their prejudices. The basic thread of any human interaction system is respect. Respect for differences in people, backgrounds, ideologies, viewpoints, etc. Being empathetic, of others' point of view is critical. Organizational climate is becoming complex by the hour. There is a lot of focus on the complexities of leadership and cultural systems – whereas sometimes the key to creating high energy work climates rests with simple human interaction systems.

There must be sensitivity training for employees and training of managers on cultural awareness and how to handle culturally diverse teams. Cultural diversity within a team can lead to increased creativity, but teams must be able to curtail cultural conflicts and focus on the common goal. Sometimes individuals are quick to feel offended by even the slightest of issues that might have happened innocently. This leads to unnecessary negativity in the workplace which might act as barriers and impede optimal performance at work. The frequency of training, as well as the type of training must be planned carefully, depending upon the unique set of circumstances. Leaders need to identify existing problem areas that may arise and how to correct them, to build and foster effective and productive teams. The understanding and acceptance of cultural differences within a team and organization is important for overall success. It is necessary to be aware of other cultures and to be respectful of their practices. On an individual level, if this approach is to be effective, managers, as well as employees, should study differences in the rituals of different cultures. In some cultures encircling the thumb and forefinger is an acceptable symbol for 'okay' whereas in other cultures it is an obscene gesture (Brazil and Iran). Additionally, you have to be very careful how you address minorities. In certain parts of the world, you may use a term to address a group, and that will be acceptable, and in another country, the same term would be considered a racial slur. Make studying of cultural, differences a habit; you and your organization will reap incredible benefits, and it may save you from unconsciously offending others or embarrassing yourself.

In AIG's 2014 corporate citizen report, it included leveraging cognitive diversity to drive innovation as a Diversity and Inclusion principle.

AIG focused its efforts on three areas in 2014:

❖ **Nomination programs.** It hosted training for 350 employees in nine countries with efforts focused on women and under-represented groups.

❖ **Training programs.** A global initiative was launched in over 20 countries to train managers in generation diversity, cultural competence, and unconscious bias.

❖ **Employee resource groups**. The enterprise's employee resource groups experienced a growth rate of 76 percent in one year. It expanded to 10 different dimensions of diversity, added to 36 existing chapters and launched 37 new groups.

4 | Promote Empowerment and participation from employees

Empowerment is power sharing. It's the delegation of authority to subordinates in the organisation. Without the participation of all members in an organisation, the goals of gaining the best that diversity brings will not be achieved. Ultimately, to better ensure that the organization's efforts towards promoting diversity is cemented, it needs to be part of the existing culture. Johnson & Johnson, the global healthcare company was listed on DiversityInc's Top 50 Companies for Diversity, eleven times. Johnson & Johnson maintains that it not only celebrates diversity — "we champion it."

Leaders should strive to manage cultural diversity by creating an environment in which the employees feel comfortable to share their differences, beliefs, visions, without fear of ridicule. It is beneficial to build a workforce in which all members understand how the other members see the world. If this can be achieved, trust, understanding, respect, and collaboration will be greatly improved. Team members will be able to better assess the needs of one another and will be able to better adjust to changes. This can be facilitated via storytelling. Managing diversity reflects understanding people's differences and viewing those differences as valuable for the organization. Encourage an organizational culture where employees are happy to share their personal stories which allows for better connection and empathy. By genuinely listening to each other, we get to appreciate different cultures and broaden our own understanding. There should be moments of team socializing so that employees can learn more about each other. Hold off-site events where employees bring their families to learn more about one another's lives' and cultures.

Companies can drive business growth and improve customer service by involving their diverse workforce. This means making use of cultural sensitivity and market knowledge of business networks in their home countries, and with these strategic assets, organisations will have competitive advantages in marketing its products to an ever growing migrant community as well as to the global market. The Avon Company was able to turn around its unprofitable inner city markets in the USA by placing Hispanic and African American managers in charge of marketing to these populations. Just as ethnic minorities may want to work for employers who value diversity, they may also want to support such organisations. Organizations need to be flexible to improvise as cultural differences arise and to evolve to better accommodate these differences. Businesses must be open to novel ideas and encourage constructive feedback and interaction. Involvement of culturally diverse teams in strategic processes such as vision-setting may be a good starting point for the organization. There must be programmes in place and resources that will help employees reduce the stress associated with feeling different. In 2016, we read a startling release by Google that 69% percent of its employees are male while 31% are female; women hold 24% of its leadership positions within the company. 59% of Google employees are white, while 32% are Asian. And Blacks and Hispanics make up only 2% and 3% respectively of their workforce. 70% percent of

Google leadership roles and 57% of tech positions are held by white employees. Google began sharing its diversity statistics in 2014, prompting other Silicon Valley giants to do the same.

5 | Embed Diversity and Inclusion as part of the Organizational Culture

Diversity inclusion involves moving beyond lip service and supporting these efforts in highly visible ways and building in accountability metrics for senior executives and managers. Diversity metrics can also be linked (directly or indirectly) to management bonuses and incentives. One of the most prevalent diversity issues in the world today is the gender pay gap. A 2015 study by the American Association of University Women found that women working full-time in the United States usually were paid 80 percent of what men were paid, a gap of 20 percent. Salesforce CEO, Marc Benioff, had a clear-cut solution when it came to doing their bit to internally resolve this. If a woman working at the company was earning less money than her male counterpart in a similar role, they would start paying her more. To get the process started, Benioff ordered an evaluation of all 17,000 employees' salaries, to compare what men made to women in comparable roles. Where there were inconsistencies, he fixed them by paying the person who was earning less more, so that their salaries were parallel to that of their peers. Roughly 6% of employees required a salary adjustment. It supposedly cost Salesforce $3 million to abolish statistically significant differences in pay. "But now we can say we pay women the same that we pay men," Benioff told those in attendance at a Fortune-hosted conference. "We looked at every single one of our female employees' salaries, and we adjusted it against all of our male employees' salaries".

Through its diversity awareness program, companies can assist individuals to understand the culture of others. Such practices will certainly help people from different cultural backgrounds to understand how to work together. Additionally, they will be better able to manage conflicts in a productive manner, so to minimise stress and negative emotions when working in a diverse workplace. Solicit assistance from the local organizations that can connect diverse candidates to businesses in your community, like recruiters, colleges and churches. Many firms have successfully adopted this method. MasterCard is partnering with INROADs, a non-profit that places high-performing Black, Latino, and American Indian students in internships at leading corporations. Dun & Bradsheet has a relationship with the National Black MBA Association (NBMBA) and is a supporter of the association's scholarship fund and outreach program.

Culture is a big buzzword in business today, mainly because businesses are finding it increasingly difficult to attract and retain young talent. Research shows that a focus on culture in both employee selection and management can have a positive impact on performance and retention. So more and more companies are asking themselves "what is the right culture of people we want to attract?" Zappos, one of the most well-known companies that values diversity did away with job postings and now focuses heavily on cultural fit. Job interviewing starts with a cultural fit interview, which carries 50% of the criteria of whether the candidate is hired. Diversity is a big part of their culture. Their philosophy is that rather than ask people to apply for a "job," they want people to apply to be part of a "team". Many companies believe that building a strong "business culture" means making everyone look the same. Zappos, on the other hand, includes "wackiness" as part of its culture, which in essence says "we respect people's uniqueness."

Maya Angelou writes of cultural difference "It is time for parents to teach young people early on that in diversity there is beauty and there is strength."

A diverse workforce should be taken as a central competency of a business because diversity in most cases is directly proportional to increased creativity and innovation. And, it is virtually true that an organization's success depends on upon its ability to embrace diversity and to harvest it in the long term. Many organizations today are actively pursuing diversity as a "business strategy." Louis Vincent Gerstner Jr. former CEO and Chairman of IBM used employee diversity as a marketing communication tool to please the diverse target audience of the brand. He defined that strategy in the following words, "We made diversity a market-based issue. It's about understanding our markets, which are diverse and multicultural." Many studies have proven that diverse teams outperform non-diverse teams and even Google has quoted MIT research which found that mixed gender teams outperform single gender teams. Karen Parkin, Chief HR Officer at the Adidas Group, succinctly portrayed the role of cultural diversity at the workplace in her following statement, "Diversity provides the steady stream of new ideas, fresh perspectives and contrary points of view that are the lifeblood of innovation." Diversity is responsible for the sustainable growth of any business. The best antidote against complacency is to make sure your workforce is diverse.

6 | Reward and Recognition

BASF a multi-national chemical company is an excellent example of a global company that introduces Diversity and Inclusion training programs to senior executives to promote diversity throughout the organization. BASF's Ambassador Network includes over 500 employees worldwide and encourages the creation of an "open corporate culture that values every individual." The company partners with the National Association of Manufacturers STEP Ahead movement to advance women in manufacturing. Additionally, the company has an advanced diversity scorecard, which measures the impact of leader behaviours on diversity outcomes. Wayne

Smith, Chairman and CEO of BASF stated, "The value of diversity and inclusion is fundamental to how we create chemistry for a sustainable future...Individuals with different backgrounds and experiences bring new ideas and perspectives to the table. Diversity makes us stronger – by leveraging our differences, we bring the best of BASF to everything we do."

Organizations should identify quantifiable measures of success. This scorecard can be useful in positively influencing the organizational culture by further demonstrating the company's keen interest in all its employees. These measurements can also be used for rewarding individuals, as well as teams for outstanding diversity management initiatives. HR would be held accountable for selecting the right individuals to begin with, as well as training and development programmes. Such measurements can be included in performance appraisals and then taken into account for determining salary increases.

7 Monitor, Measure and Modify

All change requires sustainability and accountability to be successfully implemented and become the new norm. Organizations that are most successful in achieving diversity have human resources systems and practices that hold managers and senior executives accountable for achieving diversity objectives. As the old adage goes, "What gets measured is what gets done." 65 percent of 321 executives of large global companies surveyed by Forbes Insights said they have a plan in place to recruit a diverse workforce — but only 44 percent have retention programs. This reveals an obvious gap when it comes to retaining diversity and inclusion in the workplace. A multicultural organization can better attract desirable talent. They tend to be more innovative and more effective at problem-solving which in turn generates more diverse ideas and fosters the development of better solutions. If people feel valued irrespective of their background, it can lead to increased commitment and productivity, better work relationships, and the retention of these model employees. Companies must have solutions in place to monitor and retain a talented and diverse workforce, such as employee resource groups and multicultural talent management. Mentors and role models should be in place to secure the survival of diversity programmes. Networks can provide social support and access to role models and mentors of the same gender and race/ethnicity.

New research makes it increasingly clear that companies with more diverse workforces perform better financially. McKinsey & Company has been examining diversity in the workplace for several years. It offers the following supported hypotheses that diversity helps to:

➤ Win the war for talent

➤ Strengthen customer orientation

➤ Increase employee satisfaction

➤ Improve decision making

➤ Enhance an organization's image

According to the Society for Human Resource Management **(SHRM):**

❖ Diversity initiatives can be the catalyst for a better ROI in human capital.

❖ The financial rewards of appealing to a more-diversified customer base are significant.

❖ Minorities are the majority in six of the eight largest metropolitan areas of the U.S.A

❖ The combined Black, Hispanic and Asian buying power is more than $750 billion with African Americans spending nearly $500 billion each year on goods and services; and Hispanics are the fastest growing consumer groups in the United States.

❖ Women are the primary investors in more than half of the U.S. households as they purchase 70 to 80 percent of all products.

PITFALLS ASSOCIATED WITH CULTURAL DIVERSITY

Certainly, with diversity, there are problems to overcome such as language barriers and differences in values and belief systems. There are also dangers associated with false feelings of not fitting in or not being appreciated leading to high turnover of diverse groups. Even when a company decides to address these issues, there are internal forces working against it. There may be a tendency to ignore such groups, and on the other hand, there may be a natural resistance amongst diverse groups to interact. As with most of the differences between cultures, the issue is not so much that the dissimilarities exist, but that these differences go unrecognized. Poorly managed diversity may cause severe losses to an organization. Mismanaging cultural diversity at work causes tensions between employees and employers, a loss of team productivity, a smeared corporate image and even discrimination lawsuits. Diversity needs to sustainable. It is not a one-off event that organizations embrace just to look good on reports. They must really value the contribution of those with differences. If an organization becomes known as one that ignores diverse employees, it will have a difficult time finding qualified workers when there is a limited skilled labour force.

CROSS-CULTURAL COMMUNICATION

With more than 200 languages spoken in the United States today, it is common to experience some language barriers creating communication problems. In our increasingly multicultural society, it is vital that employers and employees have the skills to communicate effectively. Managers typically see cultural diversity in the workplace as a problem to be dealt with as it takes a lot of work and is a complicated issue. Building a diverse workforce can be a daunting and complex task. Leaders have to recognise the differences and to value and optimise the unique strengths each person brings to the company. Organizations can take a closer look into educational pipelines, job training programmes, and other areas which inadvertently reduce diversity in the workforce. The overall impact of having a diverse workforce is a positive one. However, the company may have to deal with the learning curve of bringing in individuals from various cultures that they have little knowledge of. The benefits are usually seen later down the road when there is a more diverse customer base utilizing the business and its product because of the varied cultural backgrounds of its employees. Cultural and language barriers need to be overcome for diversity programmes to succeed. Ineffectual communication of important objectives results in misunderstandings, lack of teamwork, and low morale.

Communication is an essential ingredient in any organization. Poor communication results in millions of losses each year for businesses. Then diversity is added to this, posing more challenges. The quality of communication will usually be limited to that which is mutually understandable to both the sender and the receiver. Communications problems are major catalysts for cross-cultural team conflicts and project failure. "The central principle of cross-cultural communication theory is that everything one does and everything one perceives is filtered through one's cultural knowledge." (Kudirka, 2013) Speech, body language and gestures are all a part of the way that people communicate; thus these things all have varying connotations based on the cultural background of the individual interpreting them. The complexity involved in breaking down the barriers of cultural communication are far beyond the control of one person. For this reason, it is imperative to have a team of people that assist in developing diversity training and guidelines within organizations.

A manager can adapt their written and spoken communications to prevent this, for example; speak clearly and slowly, avoid slangs, use simpler language and reiterate key points. A leader should deliver criticism and praise prudently in a cross-cultural context and teach employees on the importance of pitch and tone of the voice and mannerisms when communicating. Communication is the hardest part of any cross-cultural management programme and it requires work and patience. Perception is different in each culture; hence our approach should be focused on building the unique strengths of our corporate environment. We need to listen more. We can only become smarter and more open-minded if we listen and share our view. The benefits from hearing multiple views and working with individuals with different perspectives brings solutions to everyday problems as well as distinctive ideas that can increase the level of productivity. This is a unique opportunity that requires mutual understanding, adjustment and flexibility. IT can help in managing cultural diversity at work. Communications and other management tools such as e-mail, intranet, and video conferencing can help break down language barriers as they have inbuilt translation features to ensure everyone is on the same page. Multicultural patterns may influence how individuals resolve contradictions between their cultural and organizational identities. This explains how multicultural people have different approaches and methods for addressing and managing conflicts.

Cultural values related to religion can also be a factor. Offering beef dishes to Hindus or requesting a Seventh Day Adventist work on a Saturday can be viewed as disrespectful. Why? In Hinduism the *cow* is considered a *sacred* animal and Seventh-day Adventists keep the Sabbath holy - more specifically, from sunset on Friday to sunset on Saturday. Religion has one of the strongest influences on how a person's beliefs and values. However, it is one of the subjects that managers avoid discussing with employees. It's like walking a sensitive line, a statement taken incorrectly could be deemed as bias. Therein lies the risk of one party unintentionally offending the other, destroying team spirit. Similarly, cultural values related to family and work ethic might arise as potential problem areas. An individual's values that are strongly influenced by family principles might be misinterpreted by a manager from a culture that puts the needs of the business first. Therefore hostility might develop if the perceptions are not openly discussed and understood. The cultural differences may further weaken the relationship between the employee and the manager when impacted by perceptions of unfairness. These elements make retention an important area of focus in diverse groups. This is where implementing flexi-time can be a suitable option.

In some cases, an individual from a certain culture might prefer to look the other way when unethical behaviour occurs, while management is assuming that such behaviour will be reported. Such propensities must be addressed through cultural sensitivity and awareness training. Gift giving and receiving by business leaders is not considered unscrupulous, or neither is condemned in many countries. Yet there is a small difference separating a gift from a bribe in business transactions and not all gift-giving is regarded as bribery. Again all employees must be properly guided by the values, mission and vision of the organization. Business culture is a particular set of expectations and acceptable behaviours of how people of organisations behave, communicate, interact and manage. Furthermore, the culture of the company might itself create an issue of diversity. Organizational culture can be defined as "the set of underlying values, beliefs, and principles that serve as a foundation for the organization's management system as well as the set of management practices and behaviours that both exemplify and reinforce those basic principles." (Denison, 1990). If the culture of an organization conflicts with the culture of a particular group it can lead to members of that group as well as management left feeling uncomfortable. Management may have to keep walking on eggshells as they need to bear in mind they need to be politically correct not to offend anyone. The organization may already be a cultural melting pot so changing the culture of the organization to suit every group is unlikely, therefore where there is a cultural clash this should be addressed in the cultural diversity management programme. Leaders must establish a set of best practices for their team that generally applies to all cross-cultural teams within the company. There should be a level playing field where no cultural group claims superiority over another.

A diverse workforce can provide substantial benefits to an organization which also includes adhering to legal compliance. Leaders who shun diversity are being placed in the hot seat. Novartis, a Swiss multinational pharmaceutical company was faced with a gender discrimination lawsuit filed in 2015—not the first time it has faced a suit of this kind. A $110 million lawsuit filed in March 2015 claimed a U.S. division of Novartis has continually refused female employees equal pay and promotion opportunities, five years after they was hit with a nine-figure jury verdict over similar allegations. The class action lawsuit filed in U.S. federal court stated Texas-based Alcon Laboratories Inc. which was acquired by Novartis in 2010, keeps a "boy's club atmosphere" that is antagonistic to women and prevents them from gaining leadership positions. After less than a year of litigation, Novartis agreed to pay $8.2 million to settle the collective class action lawsuit filed by more than a dozen female employees. Additionally, in 2010, a U.S. jury ordered the company to pay more than $250 million in a separate class action that claimed widespread gender discrimination. This was the largest award in an employment discrimination case in U.S. history at that time.

Aaron Slator, an AT&T executive who became the subject of a $100-million discrimination lawsuit, was fired by the company in April 2015. The lawsuit was filed by a black woman who worked under Slator. She claimed Slator embarked on a campaign to harass her after she discovered a racist meme that was sent to a friend on a work phone. In a statement, AT&T said it had fired Slator, president of content and ad sales, and regretted not doing so earlier. The statement added that "there is no place for demeaning behavior within AT&T." "A lawsuit is often a call to action and incentive to standardize or beef up procedures and training," said Luke Visconti, CEO and founder of DiversityInc. "Senior executives realize that they can no longer assume good behavior; they need to codify it. This was the case for companies like Coke, Sodexo and Novartis—and they all came out the other side as even better companies."

Although diversity is beneficial to an organization. It has drawbacks that organizations must take into consideration to ensure it is reaping the priceless benefits of "Unity in Diversity." I have seen some cases where organizations have gone over the top on diversity trying too hard and have overused the term that the spirit of real diversity gets watered down. On the other hand, you shouldn't be pressured to hire individuals to meet your diversity targets who truly are not a good fit for your organization. There must be a careful balance otherwise you will be all over the place. Additionally, if you keep only heralding diversity workers, those from the homogenous home group may feel left out. Diversity is supposed to include all people and make them feel appreciated and welcomed. Make sure you are not missing the mark or being manipulated by focusing on the loudest group who are quick to cry discrimination. Organizations can often feel trapped when dealing with attitudes of entitlement among certain minority groups. It should also be noted that, since each person has individual characteristics, cultural diversity management should regard the diverse needs of individuals.

Sadly in some organizations, I have consulted with the issue of diversity is viewed as more of a problem that has to be tolerated. They have this all-inclusive front for the watching world, but deep down they don't really value it. They see it as too much work, or that it can complicate things. Multiculturalism is often viewed as a "nice to have" in today's world however, it isn't an option as your survival may depend on it. Due to the intense competition among companies on a global scale, it is even more important for companies to be able to retain their workforce. People aspire and want to work at such as companies such as Facebook, Google, American Express, GE, McKinsey, etc. because these companies go out of their way to take great care of their employees. Therefore they recruit and retain the best talent, thus making them even better at what they do and they remain globally competitive. Multiculturalism and diversity are key drivers for entrepreneurship and innovation; to get new ideas and innovations we need a global perspective.

THE NOKIA EXAMPLE

Nokia the pioneer and Goliath in mobile phone segment fell from industry leadership in the space of less than five years. One of the reasons was due to lack of diversity. Nokia's top executives were all of similar age and backgrounds, and this contributed to their reduced ability to make sense of their changing business environment. The result was inevitable blind spots. They refused to listen to young, creative and passionate disruptors. They were overconfident and became complacent with their leadership position in the marketplace. **They engaged in groupthink** and ceased to innovate. During Stephen Elop's tenure as CEO, Nokia's stock price dropped 62%, their mobile phone market share was halved, their smartphone market share fell from 33% to 3%, and the company suffered a cumulative €4.9 billion loss. Dr. Rohini Anand of Sodexo USA said, "Inclusive leadership starts with self-awareness, being introspective, knowing your blind spots and possessing the ability to listen and learn."

Nokia's lesson is one of a sad reality and that so many companies realize after it is too late. Life is full of constant changes, challenges and adaptations. One either adapts and moves with change or remains stagnant and dies. It's survival of the fittest, strongest and most dynamic in all industries - but more so in technology, as in this industry changes are constant and trends move at staggering speed. In the late 1990s, Infosys had a programme called **"Voice of Youth" designed to bring the insights of the under-30 crowd to the attention of the 50-something executive team**. Diversity can help you stay relevant as you follow up the tide and new trends. Nokia went into denial when the iPhone appeared. They thought it was a fad and they could withstand it. Innovation makes you or breaks you and is indeed the only practical source of your competitive advantage. Lack of diversity leads to complacency. The biggest threat to success is success itself. Success breeds complacency which breeds failure.

It is difficult to simulate hunger when you are full. They got into a comfort zone and contentment set in. There is an old saying: Don't fall in love with your product. That is the hidden threat for so many companies.

"Our industry does not respect tradition, it only respects innovation"
—Satya Nadella, CEO of Microsoft

A diverse workforce brings enhanced problem solving and creativity. Diverse groups have proven to be more creative than homogenous groups, being people with various backgrounds bring multiple perspectives to the table. Amazon Founder Bezos says, "We are stubborn on vision. We are flexible on details." Nokia failed to stay ahead of the changing world while being satisfied with past successes, similar to Kodak and Blackberry. Never stop on your way of continuous improvement. Customers want a product of the future, not an outdated product. Your half-hearted efforts would not succeed. You must make an effort to not only improve the packaging but the product itself. It's a constant race, and the fastest and best will win. At one point Nokia had some of the best products but there was not enough drive for innovation to remain at the top.

A Cartoon in a magazine years ago showed a business executive in a meeting with other executives. He was holding a box of cereal in his hands, showing it to the attendees in the meeting. He pointed to the word 'New' that was in large bold letters on the box, the assumption being, the product was new. The executive then said, "It's the '**New**' on the box that is new." In other words, all that they did was simply add the word New on the box, but everything else remained the same.

To succeed, companies need to adopt new methods of conducting business, with sensitivity toward the needs of cultural practices. Embracing diversity in your organization fosters a culture of welcoming change. Change is dynamic. You either sink, or you swim. True to personal life and business, life is about continuous learning. Learn, unlearn and re-learn with an open mind and this what diversity fuels. "The only thing that is constant is change" —Heraclitus. We need to be constantly alert to changes in our different industries which is vital to adapt and to always be on top of our game. Those who refuse to take risks & improve, will one day become redundant & not relevant to the industry. If you don't learn new things daily, you will fall behind and expose you and your organization to elimination. The trends of tomorrow will displace the advantage you have today. Even the best companies with great products can be ruins in a flash of a technology shift, if not managed well. Be the change agent, lest you be swept by change. Hard lessons are often learned at a great cost.

Alfred North Whitehead (1861-1947), an influential mathematician and author, said the following: "Fifty-seven years ago it was when I was a young man in the University of Cambridge. I was taught science and mathematics by brilliant men and I did well in them; since the turn of the century I have lived to see every one of the basic assumptions of both set aside. . . . And yet, in the face of that, the discoverers of the new hypotheses in science are declaring, 'Now at last, we have certitude.' "—A. N. Whitehead, Dialogues of Alfred North Whitehead.

Nokia was disrupted. Disruption is ruthless. Keep learning, keep applying, keep imagining, keep experimenting and then...Repeat gain. "Evolve with the world," that's the catchphrase. Nokia failed to evolve and lost their chance of survival. You should never assume you will stay on top. Embrace and ride the changes or you may suffer the consequences. By taking advantage of the benefits of diversity, organizations will have further value and competitive advantages over organizations which do not embrace this business strategy. Therefore with effective management, diversity can give competitive advantages to the organization. There are many drivers as increased productivity, higher employee satisfaction, greater innovation, and improved financial performance behind diversity and inclusion. Companies that value diversity as a key strategic asset and implement and nurture it, will find themselves ahead of the competitors that do not embrace cultural diversity for the power and potential that it possesses.

CONCLUSION

In a world where "ethnic cleansing" is a present evil, leaders need to be an instrument to another set of values that do not "rate" people, by prejudices. We must realize in spite of all the differences people are very similar and most of us what the same things. We are all part of one single human family. Seek Unity rather than uniformity. Kings in ancient times always had to be cautious of the danger of an internal revolt. A ceremony would be arranged where all the officials had to show public allegiance to the king, to bring them all into line. One of the greatest challenges facing larger corporations is the question of unity. There is a continuous danger of growing apart or even fragmenting unless we develop programs to maintain and grow a genuine closeness. There shouldn't be clusters of diverse groups who don't interact with other groups - that is defeating the purpose. At times I have witnessed diverse groups that keep to themselves and exclude others. Leaders need to get these employees out of their comfort zones by switching employees work stations and also moving them around in different teams. Leaders should spread unity over divisiveness for individuals to work together as a team. It doesn't mean we must dress, speak or look alike but we value and respect each other's differences and are committed to working together for the overall success of the organization. A sustained focus on unity is, therefore, needed more than ever as we face the challenges and competition in the evolving marketplace. The organization must be characterized by unity rather than uniformity. There is beauty and richness in diversity as long as we appreciate the differences we all possess. Moving towards a collaborative approach to completing work creates a unity that is inspiring, productive, and engaging. Employers must not only see the urgency to include diversity, but they need to understand what motivates an employee's behaviours. Universally, we all want to achieve self-actualization. Self-actualization is the highest level of Maslow's Hierarchy of needs which he describes as the desire to accomplish everything that one can, to become the most that you can be. There are common motivational factors for most employees within the organization. We all want meaningful work – to know we're doing something significant and our contribution to the organization is valued. We want growth and personal development – to learn new things and feel challenged by our jobs. Ideally, this should be in an environment where we feel appreciated and respected with a team of great people that we like to work with. When employees feel empowered, they take ownership of their work which improves morale, commitment and productivity. To make diversity a life-force, it must be coupled with speaking to the hearts and aspirations of your employees. Stay focused and committed. No company creates a culture of diversity and inclusion in one leap. It can take months and even years, to form best practices, but when these are in place, your organization can reap the long-term benefits.

CHAPTER FIVE

HOW TO INCREASE TEAM PRODUCTIVITY

The total value produced by teamwork depends on the overall effectiveness of the team effort. Every company will sooner or later face a situation where team productivity plateaus. To improve productivity organizations should focus on what already works, as well as revising the areas that are causing the most disturbance.

Ten Actions for Improving Team Productivity:

1 **Keep teams small.** One of the best methods to getting things done quickly is through having a small team. Efficiency is all about having a purpose, clear direction, defined goals and involving as few people as possible. Dividing a complex task into smaller and simpler parts, is the key to keep teams small. Small teams are be able to conduct meeting and brainstorming better than big ones. According to author Stephen Robbins, when teams have more than 10-12 people, the team finds constructive interaction difficult. I have seen a team of 20 perfectly capable individuals be less productive than a team of 5 persons. You can see the effects of this in successful start-ups all the time - a small group of people focused on getting an inordinate result. It's worth referring to the Ringelmann Effect (1913) where the force on a rope pulled by different sizes of teams were measured. When solving for the average effort made by people at different team sizes, Ringelmann observed that the bigger the team, the less each member pulled. Keeping teams small may keep average effort up.

2 **Create a better physical work environment.** We're all affected by our physical environment. Productivity can fall or rise depending on how we feel. A poorly lit or dull workspace can sap our energy, while a disorganized or distracting space can limit our ability to focus. Create the best working environment possible. Team members will appreciate this, and it may not only improve overall productivity but also well-being.

3 **Team Coaching** is the most direct method when you want the people in your organization to develop into high-performing teams. Recent research suggests some teams fail because their members are not prepared for the transformation from

individual contributor to team member. Coaching is focused on improving their ability to function effectively as a team. Once everyone is entirely clear about the goals, directions and their role in contributing to the overall success of the team, it's time to teach team members how to work together. For a team to perform well together, members need to have the necessary skills to interact with one another. Everyone should know the essentials of effective collaboration; including a variety of relationship and communication skills so that they are able to put forward their suggestions, listen to other members' ideas as well as quickly resolve conflicts. You can observe the team while the team is doing work to see patterns of interaction and to get a sense of the group dynamics. At the end of a real work session, you should have a meeting to go over what you have observed during their exchanges. Coaching is beneficial to encourage them to share feedback and information, challenge their assumptions, limit non-helpful behaviours and to show them how to reduce conflict while encouraging their commitment to achieving results. It's also important to also dedicate the time to jointly review their progress in a structured format. This will also give them the opportunity to address real work challenges. You will need to listen to every team member with the same attention as you do when you are coaching just one individual. The team works on problems through facilitated discussions and commits to action based on insights gained. Effective team coaching requires you to rise above the dynamics of the group and observe what is going on. The capacity to be separate from, yet part of, the dynamics of the group is a form of constructive detachment that prevents you from taking sides or becoming caught up in the feelings of the group.

4 | Improve Standards and Processes. **Host a workshop on the common productivity killers** to help your team identify what activities takes the most time away from their daily routine. Any systematic approach to improving performance needs to challenge existing habits of working. Ask team members how tasks can be simplified and to re-examine their to-do lists, in order to ensure that they are always working on what is most important. There may be specific tasks that take up considerable time and aren't necessarily relevant or critical to the success of the business. Leaders should consider how they can restructure processes to allow their teams to spend more time doing what matters. Your team could have ideas on how to increase productivity. They might have given thought to how efficiency can be improved. Furthermore, teach them how to build better work habits. Regularly assess your team's performance, efficiency and effectiveness. You should spend time towards improving workflows by using simple tools as checklists, reflection and feedback.

5 | Be Available. Work with your teams. A good leader works with the team as one, respects his/her team members, motivates them, and is there to provide support. The teams' success is your success. You have to remember to adjust to their priorities depending on their capabilities while pushing them to grow and

achieve more. You can't expect an underperforming employee to exceed high targets; it will put too much pressure on them and negatively affect their job satisfaction level. Ensure individuals have received adequate training and the necessary resources and make yourself available to give advice and guidance. If you are empathetic and make your team feel valued, then you'll be instilling trust and commitment in your team.

6 **Manage input.** Information overload impedes productivity. To give meaningful direction, there's only so many ideas an individual can mentally handle. Quite often people aren't looking for choice; they're looking for the right solution. Have a system for filtering suggestions in your team. Adopt the process of selectivity to decipher and consolidate input. For example, eliminate choices to remain at the top 7 or 20%. This sharpens the team's focus and creativity. You can get stuck by the abundance of ideas and the sheer volume of available data.

7 **Provide the Proper Tools** – A team will be more productive when they have the necessary resources and appropriate tools for the job. Understandably, there can be budget constraints, however not providing the proper tools is unacceptable. I worked with a financial company that would not allow staff any software that was not approved by the Information Technology department. Therefore to get any additions to the approved list took tiers of authorization which was extremely difficult to get, in a timely fashion.

8 **Remove Roadblocks** – Removing hindrances is one of the main functions of a leader. Your team will encounter problems that hinder their progress. Your job is to eradicate obstacles that keep them from efficiently getting their work done. Teams must have clear pathways to work smoothly and be able to implement their decisions with confidence. A recent example was a team

that was getting kicked out of the office for being there after work hours. Management was not supportive of late hours access to the workplace. After putting together a strong case, management eventually authorized permission for controlled entry. In this case, the programming team did some of their best work late in the evenings when the office was vacant.

9 **Reserve downtime. Encourage breaks.** This may sound counterproductive, but it really works. You can't run continually for 8 hours, and neither can your team. If your organization has a hard- driving culture, you should consider authorizing breaks for your team. Research shows that anticipated time off improves productivity and morale. Stopping for a 10 - 15 minute break from all work gives you time to rest your mind, shake off sluggishness, recharge and jump back into your routine with full force thus functioning at 100 percent.

10 **Improve the way you run meetings.** Meetings are a great way to keep in touch and stay up to date with what is happening in an organization, but they can be very time consuming and unproductive as they interrupt a steady work-flow. Free up your team by eliminating unnecessary meetings. Meetings are good to keep people informed. If you do have regular meetings, keep it short. Some organizations have regular Stand Up Meeting or 'SUM' for short. This is a short daily meeting in which members say which tasks were completed the previous workday, and what they will be working on in the present day. These meetings should be very concise—no more than 15 minutes. Meetings in general, should never be scheduled without a purpose and an agenda. Only invite people who need to be involved. Make sure everyone gets the agenda prior to the meeting and request they come with facts. In conversations, get to the point, remain on topic and insist that others do the same. Action items should be written down to allow team members to leave with a specific

plan of action on how to proceed forward. **Time management** is an overlooked key to success. Promote consistency and respect for each other's' time by sticking to finishing times.

"Productivity is never an accident. It is always the result of a commitment to excellence, intelligent planning, and focused effort." — Paul J. Meyer

Productivity can also be improved by **team alignment, instilling a sense of urgency and improving team morale.** In this section we will look closer at these three essential areas.

The Importance of Team Alignment to Achieve Peak Performance

How often have you worked with a team that isn't on the same page? This situation of being misaligned is not the team's fault but the responsibility of the leader/manager. Teamwork is fundamental

to success, and 97% of executives, employees and educators responding to a recent Fierce.com poll said a lack of team alignment impacts the outcome of tasks or projects.

"The most empowering condition of all is when the entire organization is aligned with its mission, and people's passions and purpose are in sync with each other." — Bill George

An employee can be engaged without being aligned. Just think of a car whose engine and transmission are both working fine. However, the wheel alignment is off, so steering becomes harder as there is the tendency to pull to one side. Regular wheel alignment inspections can help protect the life of a vehicle's tires while enhancing vehicle safety. Just as alignment plays a critical role in the performance of your vehicle, it also does in the performance of your team. Even in nature alignment matters. When birds fly in a V-formation, this is to boost the efficiency and range of the flying birds, particularly over long migratory routes. Geese in a V-formation may conserve 12–20% of the energy they would need to fly alone. The formation also makes communication easier and allows the birds to maintain visual contact with each other. In the business world, alignment is when the entire organization is in sync with the company's vision, mission, and strategic plan and there are clear expectations of roles and responsibilities. Research states that 90% of organizations fail to successfully implement their strategies. This is based on Gartner, Inc. the prediction for 2018 is still at 90%. Organizational alignment begins with team alignment. Team alignment is about taking the intrinsic motivations of the team and aligning them with the goals of the organization. It ensures your team is focused and going in the right direction. Team alignment is a critical success factor found in high performing teams. The purpose of team alignment is to help your team build a plan of action that is consistent with the organization's goals.

Generating real alignment requires considerable effort. Alignment rarely evolves naturally. Various circumstances including a change in strategic direction, new leadership, an acquisition, etc., and other scenarios can result in teams falling out of sync. Leaders should be determined to figure out if the team is aligned. While everyone may be nodding their heads in agreement around the table, what happens outside the meeting room is more telling. Aligned teams have a high level of clarity and agreement on their purpose, objectives, roles and values.

One way to determine the degree of alignment within the leadership team would be to ask each member to answer the following four questions:

- ❖ **Why are we here?** This basically answers what the team is there to accomplish. Is everyone clear about this? Your team's mission statement is the foundation to alignment. The purpose of the team must be clearly defined and communicated.

- ❖ **Where are we heading?** Your direction may be your strategic goals or your operational objectives. Goals must be quantifiable rather than vague. So for example, a goal to "Build better customer relationships" is not clear enough. By contrast, "Increase re-order rates by 60%" is specific.

- ❖ **Who does what**? Is everyone aware of each other's roles and responsibilities? The key is clarity and simplicity. Assign roles based on team members' strengths.

- ❖ **What are our Core Values**? Do team members approach the workload with similar values or comparable commitment and passion? Having an understanding of the team's core values can help reduce conflict. An example of team values could include, Honesty, Excellence, Accountability, Respect, Commitment, Be Creative and Open-Minded, Embrace and Drive Change, Be Passionate and Determined, etc.

If a team comes back with a dozen different answers to the above questions, they are clearly misaligned and not on the same page. The results will help you to determine what needs fixing. Meet with the team collectively to communicate why there is a need for team alignment and where the misalignment is. Clarify purpose, goals, roles and values where necessary. Alignment has a direct impact on growth and performance and is an important factor in an organization's ability to build and maintain a culture of innovation, speed and flexibility. When a team is in alignment, every member is highly committed and gives their all to achieving the team's goals. **An old Ethiopian proverb states that when spider webs unite, they can tie up a lion**. The efforts of one person combines and build on the efforts of another, and the output often surpasses the sum of the individual inputs. Without alignment around the team purpose, the result is loss of efficiency and productivity.

Instilling a Sense of Urgency

All teams can become more productive. Teams that are cohesive and comfortable with each other may get laid-back as they feel safe in their current state - so you want to keep the energy high. This means creating a sense of urgency. Bear in mind a sense of urgency does not mean frantic, anxious activity 24/7. It's rather engaged urgency that drives people to move ideas swiftly along the production line from talking to action. Instilling a sense of urgency, unless handled with care, could develop into a toxic misunderstanding between employees and management with staff seeing this as something leading to higher stress levels. Urgency should be a natural result of sharing a sense of purpose. **Your team needs to move with a sense of urgency. This doesn't mean moving fast. It means moving with purpose.**

> "The companies that thrive in today's economy will be those that can shift their cultures from the slower pace of business-as-usual to urgency."—Michael Hyatt

7 Ways to Increase Urgency

➢ **Communicate a sense of urgency-** Take the time to let your team know why a sense of urgency is important in each given situation. Share the importance of completing a given task on time. Clarify the consequences of inaction. Don't exhibit panic, stress or loss of control. Help your team understand why it matters to do their collective best.

➢ **Be Transparent -** Share not only good news but bad news as well with the organization. Make sure that transparency is part of the culture. When your team knows what the real stakes are for your business, it helps them to give more at their jobs. Your team members will step up and take more responsibility when you're honest with them about finances, clients, and expectations. If you hide aspects of the situation from your team, they can't help you come up with innovative solutions to problems.

➢ **Get Customer Feedback** - This prevents your team from operating in a vacuum and requires managers and employees to talk to unhappy customers and suppliers and address their comments placed in the suggestion boxes to directly understand and resolve their concerns. As the marketing rule of thumb states: For every person who takes a moment to complain to a business, there are at least ten more customers who are just as angry but don't take the time to voice their objections.

➢ **Open Question and Answer Forums** - No matter how well you try to communicate, there will always questions and misunderstandings that come up. It's important to include a regular group forum where any questions and concerns can be raised and addressed. An effective way to do this is through the "I Like, I Wish, I Wonder" feedback process developed at the Stanford's d.school. The concept is simple. The team members stand in a circle and discuss the past week. The only rule is that each person must start his or her statement with "I like…", "I wish…" or "I wonder…" Keep the remarks brief. Additionally, any topic of interest is fair game.

➢ **Act on Ideas** – Don't just keep discussing and analyzing decisions over and over trying to develop the perfect plan. The point of total certainty never comes. Make a decision to do something. Set the example. Make smart decisions with confidence and act on them quickly. As the old adage goes, "it is easier to steer a moving object." If you make a blunder, you can adjust. But if you take too long, you'll totally miss the opportunity. In today's fast paced technology driven environment speed can be a competitive advantage. However, it requires leaders who are willing to push themselves and their teams into motion.

➢ **Keep the ball rolling** – Minimize bureaucratic paperwork. Identify obstacles and remove them fast. After you get started, keep things moving with a focus on completion. Do things quickly. Create an atmosphere of movement and action. Whether dealing with a small problem or a big one, everyone needs to respond as though it matters. Establish an outcome-focused culture (instead of task-focused). Celebrate successes more often. If you follow all the bureaucratic red tape but don't accomplish your goals, you have failed. Results are the goal.

➢ **Evaluate** – To produce results faster means figuring out what works and what doesn't. Remove the indecisive actions that slow your team down. If the current plan of action is not moving the team toward the desired outcome, be quick to change strategies and include something else.

Improve Team Morale:
Create a comfortable company culture

Many managers complain about heavy workload & limited time. Teamwork is the path to achieving more in less time. Culture is the glue that holds the team together. A strong office culture can result in heightened motivation, increasing overall organizational effectiveness. Teams need to feel positive about their organization and the tasks they are performing to remain as productive as possible. Company culture is shaped through your daily work customs; habits that set the behavioural and social norms that go onto enhancing your company's unique personality. It's important to **build team spirit.** This goes beyond your immediate team. Make everyone feel as though "we're in this together." Improving your business culture requires regular work. It takes a little effort to get going, but after a while, you won't notice how easy developing your culture becomes.

Here are 8 Things a company can do to Improve Morale.

1 Create a Company Culture Manifesto

Most companies have mission statements, which is great, but manifestos are better. A manifesto is a clear and public declaration of purpose and intent and captures the guiding philosophy of the organisation. Mission and vision statements are written for the boardroom and can seem cold. On the other hand, manifestos are written with the employee and customer in mind and at heart. When done right, a manifesto not only inspires employees but customers and attracts future talent.

AAPT, Australia's leading telecommunications carrier, company Manifesto:

"We're a David in a world of Goliaths. A world that's complicated, cluttered and confusing. We have chosen not to accept the lousy and low standards of our category. We boldly believe the best stone we can throw is the stone of simplicity. To simply make it easier. To simply make the complex clearer. To simply make AAPT the easiest to choose and the easiest to use. To simply be a breath of fresh air, a better option, in a zoo of choice. We believe better communication makes for a better life. Communication lies at the heart of everything we do. However we choose not to make the industry's complexity the customers problem. We choose common sense over complexity. We can make a difference. We will simply work smarter to find better ways, to find better solutions, to set a whole new standard. A standard called simplicity. We know we can be that bold. We know how the story ends. BOLD SIMPLICITY"

| 2 | Create a "Vision Board"

The vision board is a collection of pictures and short idioms that represent your business goals. The purpose of a vision board is to get a company focused on what it is striving for. It is a roadmap to where you want to go. This powerful device serves as your model of the future. Pictures and images will stimulate emotion and strengthen resolve to passionately pursue the vision. It also helps to keep a team focused on achieving goals. People are visual learners and as the saying goes, "A picture paints a thousand words," without a doubt holds true. Vision boards should focus on the desired goal and always be positive. Additionally, make the creation of a vision board a team activity and keep it in a high traffic location.

| 3 | Give some Stand Out Perks

A paycheck isn't the only thing that makes employees happy. Stand out perks are a great way to communicate to your team that you value and care about them. Here are 3 companies with some great stand out perks:

- ❖ Google is known for free meals, recreational activities, a gym, and on-site massages.

❖ Cisco Systems - Cisco has an on-site fitness centre, physical therapy and acupuncture.

❖ S.C. Johnson offers a concierge service to help employees with their personal errands such as picking up dry cleaning and returning library books.

Although standard benefits are still an important part of employee satisfaction, there are some modern workplace perks that are engaging and encouraging to employees. Great employee perks focus on fostering a culture of health and wellness, a flexible work environment and support for the family dynamic. It doesn't always take an extensive budget to make and keep employees happy. Some of these perks are very simple to implement and don't cost a fortune.

4 | Show n' Tells

Weekly show n' tells, where all team members are encouraged to display what they did in the week, can play a major role in building a tight-knit team. Show n' tells cultivate strong pride in individuals and increase team members contributions to achieving goals. It increases open feedback, allows team members to be aware of each other's work and serves as a form of recognition.

5 | Lunch and Learns.

A Learn at Lunch programme is a training event scheduled occasionally during the lunch period. It is usually less formal and less structured than usual training activities. Invite speakers into the office to inspire people and educate them. This doesn't have to be done on a big budget. You can ask your employees for topics they are interested in and get talented staff to talk in areas they're skilled in and passionate about. Typical Learn at Lunch training programmes include product training, employee-led professional development, personal development and life skills.

6 **Send 'Applause'**

Promote a culture of appreciation by encouraging employees to send a thank you message to colleagues and teams. An Applause can be sent when an individual or a team has gone out of their way to help someone. The person or team with the most Applause a month gets a prize. However, this needs to be properly controlled. I have worked in companies where employees send thank yous for trivial personal things which were non-work related.

7 **Introduce a 'Dare to Try' Award.**

This is critical to letting people experiment and grow. Responsibility can be demotivating if the consequences of error or failure are too great. Having an award to celebrate an idea whether it succeeds or fail is an excellent way to let people know that new ideas are encouraged. Credit goes to Tata group who started this in 2007 to promote a culture of 'risk taking'. For a company to get ahead of the competition, it needs to innovate which involves taking risks. Risks can lead to hits and misses. Although failure is never the goal of a company, failure gets you closer to perfecting ideas and is better than not trying in the first place.

8 | Have Fun - Create and cast a company play

Creating a play acted out by your team is a fun way to get people to cooperate. I have to say I especially enjoy this one. It can be used as a great icebreaker to start a meeting. Your team can act out scenarios of job tasks, company policies, customer concerns and even do role plays with the aim of addressing and educating everyone on resolving current issues. This can be very interesting as it is done in a way for the team to remember the lessons learnt plus it allows the personalities of everyone involved to shine.

When you have a high level of team adeptness and cohesiveness, you ultimately work smarter and can accomplish more. Trusting your people and seeing them sacrifice for each other and for the sake of the team is what it's all about. Productivity is the positive by-product of this equation. Teams will be more committed when individuals feel the team is more important than self. An organization of these types of teams will achieve great things.

CHAPTER SIX

Teamwork and Collaboration: Using Synergy to Make 1 + 1 = 3

Sometimes the nature and complexity of some tasks make it almost impossible for one person alone to effectively complete a task. The benefits of teamwork are far and widespread. Teamwork helps accomplish more goals, it fosters creative ideas and solves problems. Teamwork can achieve more in a company than each one of us working alone because there is power not only in numbers but in being part of a team.

"Talent wins games, but *teamwork* and intelligence wins *championships.*" —*Michael Jordan*

Benefits of Teamwork

> **Increases Efficiency**: Teamwork blends and maximizes complementary strengths thus bringing out the best in each team member. Teamwork creates outcomes that make better use of resources and produce richer ideas. When people synchronize their efforts, they can divide up roles and tasks to more thoroughly address concerns and issues. A collaborative effort from a group of people will help create a better workflow and allow tasks to be completed faster. It enables sharing of expertise. With more hands on deck, problems can be solved quicker, and tasks can be completed more efficiently. There is higher quality output as the strengths of each team members is capitalized.

> **Encourages Creativity and Innovation**: More thoughtful ideas: A great team is made up of diverse members. A group can sometimes deal with complicated and difficult problems more effectively than individuals can. With more minds and different skills being applied to the same problem, you can come up with more practical solutions to problems than one person working on the same problem. Working as a team also encourages healthy risk taking. Trusting your teammates provides a feeling of security that allows ideas to emerge. Individuals are more likely to take risks when they experience the safety of being part of a high performing team as they have the support of the entire group to fall back on in case of failure.

➢ **Better Employee Relations** - Good teamwork maximizes involvement and participation of members. By utilizing teamwork, an organization's decision-making process can be more transparent and better understood by its members. New processes can be more easily introduced with employees having a sense of involvement. Employees that connect directly with their workplace will more likely remain with the company.

➢ **Improves Service**: When everyone is on the same page and putting the interest of the team and organization first, they will automatically want to improve service to internal and external customers and stakeholders.

➢ **Learning and Growth**. Great teamwork requires communication, cooperation, collaboration, and commitment. Teamwork provides team members with the opportunity for learning and professional development. Information is shared amongst team members, making the most of the levels of knowledge and learning for the whole organization. It also teaches members conflict resolution skills. When conflict arises, employees are forced to resolve the conflicts themselves instead of running to management.

➢ **Reduces Stress**: Being a member of a great team can reduce stress; the workload is shared, the burden will be lighter. This helps to prevent burnout. When employees find joy in their work, and they experience increased job satisfaction and less stress, companies see higher engagement levels.

➢ **Promotes the sense of accomplishment, equity and camaraderie.** When members of a team work to accomplish specific goals, there is often a greater sense of achievement than what an individual may feel when working on their own.

This combined with a sense of belonging and appreciation can significantly improve team spirit.

> **Improves motivation and morale**. When an organization encourages collaboration and cooperation, strong relationships are developed among co-workers. As people communicate and get to know each other, camaraderie is established. This can lead to improved employee morale as the team gains more ownership over the projects they are working on. People are more emotionally positive when they have shared goals. Because team members can rely on other people with shared goals, they can receive support and reassurance as they work on tasks. It also gives individuals an interest in encouraging and aiding other members of the team to achieve those shared goals. This mutual support can be quite encouraging since knowing if you fall or get stuck there is someone who has your back. It's a great feeling. It helps employees open up and encourage each other. This can inspire people to achieve goals they may not have realized they could reach on their own.

"The nice thing about teamwork is that you always have others on your side."—Margaret Carty

TEAM COLLABORATION

Many projects do not deliver desired results and get cancelled before they are completed. Ineffective team collaboration is one of the primary contributors to failure and costly rework in many projects. Collaboration is the action of working together to produce an outcome. The dictionary definition of collaboration is a - Cooperative arrangement in which two or more parties (which may or may not have any previous relationship) work jointly towards a common goal. Collaboration is a big issue for teams which are located in one place, and it becomes a huge problem for virtual teams which have team members spread across different geographical locations.

In today's business world IQ and EQ are necessary but no longer sufficient. It's time to raise our collaborative intelligence, our CQ, in business. –Marshall Goldsmith

Collaboration versus Teamwork

Teamwork and collaboration are often used interchangeably but there are some noticeable differences. Teamwork defines a group of people working together to achieve a common goal, but each individual within the team may be doing a different activity to assist the group. Whereas, collaboration is a type of teamwork that requires two or more people to work closely to achieve a goal. They work together by feeding off one another. Collaboration involves jointly producing an output. Collaboration is more interdependent and requires excellent group communication and interpersonal skills. Teams can often still do well without these qualities by way of good team leader. However, to be successful in today's world, teams need to collaborate effectively. Collaboration is about creating a sense of community and fostering a family atmosphere. Collaborators need to be emotionally engaged with each other. **You wouldn't collaborate with a stranger**. We need to look beyond teamwork and a single goal. We need to encourage people to share their knowledge with individuals beyond their immediate team for the business to develop its strategic advantage.

In order to collaborate, we have to communicate, and email is not the most effective means of communication. We don't live in the stone ages anymore. New technologies are available & inexpensive which significantly help with team collaboration. There are many cloud software out there that can help you create projects, share documents online, assign and share tasks, track the team's progress, add milestones, handle events, etc. Cloud computing can help your business accomplish more in less time by working from anywhere allowing you to be mobile while still having access to essential files and tools. According to a recent poll on Twitter, 41% of business owners agree that team collaboration is the top benefit of the cloud. Cloud computing is the practice of using a network of remote servers hosted on the Internet to store, manage, and process data, instead of your local server or your computer's hard drive. David Smith, Microsoft's VP of Worldwide Small Business Sales shared a case study about Holwick Constructors in a recent Twitter chat. According to Smith, the organization was spending around 12 hours on IT weekly. But when it started using the cloud for team collaboration, all that regained time led to an estimated $2 million in extra business. According to another tweet from Smith, 44 percent of small business proprietors surveyed stated that cloud and mobile technology have led to improved satisfaction among their customers.

Harvard Business Review study concluded, "The time spent by managers and employees on collaborative activities has ballooned by 50% or more." To foster an environment of collaboration. You must create dependencies; organise work and processes (whenever possible) so that success can only be achieved by people working together. Share resources -Try to make at least two to three people work on a certain type of task periodically. Furthermore, design remuneration and reward systems to reward team performance. Individual performance appraisal ratings should factor in a person's collaborative working skills.

Synergy = 1+1 = 3

Synergy is so popular online that it brings up 51,800,000 results. The first known use of 'synergy' was in *1632*. Spelled synergie, the word referred to the cooperation between human will and divine grace. The concept of synergy in organizations was prominent during the 1990's. During which takeovers and mergers sold the idea of cost and other savings and benefits through *synergistic action.* It's interesting to note that the current understanding of synergy is a scientific one proposed by chemists. Synergy is when two forces come together and do something much greater than they can individually.

In 2014, if you saw the look on Lionel Messi's face when he was receiving the FIFA *Golden Ball* for the best player of World Cup *2014*. Was he happy? No. He looked rather disappointed. Why? His team lost. He was disappointed his team lost despite his golden ball moment. Sadly though, one star player cannot catapult a team to success. The FIFA Soccer World Cup, occurring every four years, is more than just about watching an excellent display of soccer talent or the spectacle and gala of the event, it speaks to what teamwork and team chemistry is all about. How about the fact that the powerhouses like Italy, Portugal, and Spain were eliminated in the Group Stage? The challenge is that team coaches have the problem of trying to instil a team chemistry in a team that plays together sporadically for the four years in between the World Cups and may have a talented superstar that wants to shine.

Most organizations that I have worked with have the same issue. There are multiple departments, but those offices hardly interact. The marketing department doesn't talk to the finance department, the finance department doesn't talk to the IT department and so on; only when they want something done. Teamwork is about continuous collaboration. It's great when organizations can develop cross-functional teams. It starts by connecting with everyone to break through functional barriers. Each team has a different strength, and this is where collaboration is essential; you can then call on each respective strength for each project or task. Teamwork is bringing everyone together. It's about developing behaviour, skills and a great working environment. Your aim is to have motivated team members who work together as efficiently as possible and to retain them. Research proves that longer the same team stays together whether it is a sports team or a string quartet the better they perform. When people better understand what others know, belief, choose and are sensitive about, they can anticipate more on the behaviour of others (Huber, 2010).

As human beings, we live in association with other human beings. Even nature shows we are meant to exist in relationships. Deep in every heart lies a longing for companionship. Someone with whom we share ideals and plans; someone who inspires us to be our best and achieve the most we can. Everyone needs someone with whom they can share confidences, enjoyments, and sorrows. In the organizational setting, teamwork fosters relationship building and fulfils this desire. For starters, most of us are here only because of a relationship that resulted in our birth. Everything we do in life involves teamwork in some form —family, marriage, church and work. And these teams are unavoidable – there is no easy discharge once the final project is complete. Their power lies in their abilities to work together— making the best use of strengths and using these to complement the weaknesses of others. These 'projects' can be anything from planning a function to planning a workshop, but our lives are made up of them. Mountaineers tied to one another with ropes, depend on teamwork to climb steep cliffs. Without this, they will not make much progress. The organization's objectives are accomplished by the input of multiple individuals with different perspectives, skills and background. Although these individuals have unique experiences, team synergy plays a vital role because it combines the different parts into a whole. Lack of synergy can affect the growth of any organization because the individuals are not on the same page or united toward the same effort. Team synergy is an essential component of performing superbly in group tasks. When everyone is focused on achieving the same outcome this is what creates synergy.

Plutarch, a Greek historian of the first century, tells how Scilurus, on his deathbed, gave a bundle of darts to each of his children and told them to try to break the darts as a unit within the bundle. However, none of the children could do so. Hence he taught them that if they held together, they would remain strong. But if they became divided, they would be weak. Working together as a team can solve many problems and create a strength no one person could ever have alone.

"Individually, we are one drop. Together, we are an ocean." — Ryunosuke Satoro

In a motor spare parts company, was facing a lack of synergy in its operations. The sales representatives were telling customers that products were out of stock based on information received from the warehouse attendants when in fact they were in stock. Many times after they told the sales representatives certain parts were not in stock, the warehouse attendants would call the customer and advise them it was in stock so the client would resubmit an order and they would receive the commission. The warehouse attendants and the sales representatives were not on the same page. Everyone was basically looking out for themselves. The company was the losers of this practice as sometimes the customer had already put through an order at a competitor. There was no sense of team spirit. The solution was to engage these two departments in ongoing team building exercises designed at growing camaraderie and fostering teamwork. The company also restructured the commission system to include both groups within the same plan. Left unchanged, this practice could destroy a company. Instead of focusing on individual efforts, now everyone was focusing on team efforts. A team has got many players, each with different strengths and weaknesses but it's the synergy that is created with all of them working together towards a common goal that gives them power. Synergy is a result of establishing trust within the team. There's something about knowing that you need one another to achieve the target and that creates a bond.

Synergistic Organizations

> Teamwork is so important that it is virtually impossible for you to reach the heights of your capabilities or make the money that you want without becoming very good at it.— Brian Tracy

As organisations, we should not only be looking at how important the individual is but rather how that person's skills can be used to complement the group. A sports team star players, often think they can do it on their own and in the case of football, they often try to make a premature shot on goal and miss ignoring the teammate who is closer to the goal. Why? It's because they want the glory and the goal added to their name. **To be effective, we sometimes have to pass the ball**. In our organizations, a superstar cannot sustain his/her efforts without the help of a winning team. Ultimately, a leader's success is based largely on the success of others. I have seen plenty of individuals who are retained in companies because they have skills that the organization thinks matters, despite being poor team members. The results are individual employees who do not act as a team.

In January 2017, Usain Bolt *was* stripped of one of his Olympic relay (men's 4 x 100m) gold *medals* won at the at the 2008 Beijing Olympics after his Jamaican teammate Nesta Carter tested positive for a banned substance. One bad action and the whole team suffered through no fault of their own. Each member had to return their medals. The action of one individual can bring down a company or uplift it. In an age of social media, individual employee actions can have dire effects on an organization. Video accounts of poor customer service experienced by a consumer can go viral on Facebook with similar hashtags on Twitter calling for a boycott of the company. This story can then be picked up by mainstream news bringing negative press. For a company to be successful everyone has to be doing the right thing. An organization cannot be successful if team members are adopting unfair practices. The reality is, we win together and we fail together!

Six Volkswagen executives were criminally charged in January 2017, for their role in the company's 2015 emission scandal. The company is set to pay $4.3 billion in criminal and civil penalties in connection with the federal investigation, bringing the total cost in the United States, including settlements of suits by car owners, to $20 billion — one of the costliest corporate scandals in history.

Every team member is important. Build an awesomely supportive culture that isn't dependent on stars & heroes. The strong team ethic & player engagement in a common goal is what separates high-performing teams from average teams. It doesn't happen overnight but through daily practice. A relay team wants to win track-and-field trophies - this is possible only with a high level of commitment, hard work and participation on the part of the members. A sports team needs all its players in order to be competitive. A company needs all its employees on board to be successful. A symphony orchestra needs every single player. For your business to operate at its maximum potential, there needs to be effective collaboration, cohesion, and team synergy. This is not to say that team members will not have disagreements at times, or that their wants and needs won't change over time however, leaders must find the team's rhythm and work to fine-tune it to ensure everyone is in sync. Synergy is one of those words. There's something about it; but what's amazing to see it come to life. Looking at such a team can be likened to listening to a symphony orchestra perform. When a single musician plays one instrument in an orchestra arrangement, the audience member may question if the notes could ever make great music. A single note held over several measures can seem to make no sense. But when the master conductor brings the orchestra in unison, blending the parts of the many performers; those seemingly random notes merge to create music that stirs the soul—a spectacular masterpiece of exquisite melody. We may not be able to see the overall plan, but if we trust our leaders and play our part, our efforts will blend with the other parts into one perfect whole.

Similarly, in a successful organization, every team member knows their roles and duties, completes their share of the workload, is committed to contributing to the success of the team, gives their best and collaboratively sees the whole process through to completion. As one of the well-known acronym for team states: "Together Everyone Achieves More." I once looked at about a large crowd of ants carrying a small branch. By itself, one ant would never be able to move this object. The ants linked together, creating a forceful chain to transport the branch. In the kingdom of the ants, cooperation is the way to success. They are not afraid of the magnitude of the tasks because everyone is working together to get the job done. They help each other making it possible for them to achieve their goals. *Ants are organized and* focus more on the needs of the colony than their individual needs. They also prepare for rainy days. If these insects can instinctively cooperate to achieve great feats, why can't we human beings who supposedly are of much higher intelligence perform likewise?

Organization equals survival. A honeybee colony requires an organized structure for survival. The queen lays the eggs that hatch into worker bees. The worker bees do all the chores, including gathering nectar and pollen, cleaning empty cells, and fanning fresh air into the hive. When you have synergy your team will move from making comments as "This isn't my real job", "It won't work", "I won't or I don't want to" to "We can do this", "It's possible" and "We've got this."

According to insurance estimates, 30 percent of all business failures are attributable to internal theft. Nearly 10 percent of employees steal on a regular basis, taking three times as much as shoplifters, making consumer prices skyrocket.

Imagine how much we could really achieve if we work as a team. Nothing in this world can be achieved without teamwork; the unconditional sharing of one's best skills and talents to benefit the group. The load may seem heavy, the task daunting, but it's collaboration and cooperation that brings and sustains success. Leaders need to place more emphasis on recognizing and rewarding Team Performance rather than individual performance. We need to move away from this culture of mainly recognizing 'star players.' Once this is implemented, it will foster a culture of teamwork. Let me clarify, when I state move away from individual to team performance I am not advocating for deindividuation. Deindividuation is when people lose their sense of individual identity when they are part of a large group or crowd. It leads to a herd type mentality as often seen in in riots or acts of vandalism carried out by groups. The reason for this is that individuals in these group settings tend to lose some of their own self-awareness and subsequent self-restraint when in groups which can have devastating effects. **We hire individuals for their individual capacity to contribute and recognize their uniqueness while promoting they merge into a team.** Teamwork must be in the heart and run through the veins of the organization. Additionally, you need to model this belief of teamwork in your working relationships with the leadership and management teams showing employees that Teamwork is valued and it is the only path to achieving goals.

"Coming together is a beginning; keeping together is progress; working together is success."—Henry Ford

In this modern, information intensive, technology driven age, you need to focus on boosting the spirit of camaraderie, of shared purpose and social cohesion in your organization. It is one of the single most important factors in how your company adapts to threats and exploits new opportunities. One you have adopted the strategy in the earlier chapters and have worked on and consistently keep working on team building, engagement and diversity inclusion - synergy will follow. It's also important to remember that synergy, like Rome, wasn't built in a day. It may take a little time to truly get to know each other and bring out the best in each other. But when you do, team synergy will have a tremendous impact on your productivity and overall bottom line. You'll ace that presentation and win that new business pitch. And the next time your team is up to complete a task, you'll feel better and stronger than before. To quote Aristotle, "The whole is greater than the sum of its parts." Where synergy abounds, people are engaged, motivated, and want to be part of the winning team and this is the culture leaders should strive to maintain in their organizations.

Great leaders make sure that the work doesn't end with them. They realize the vision is so great that it might not be attained in their lifetime, so they train, mentor, teach and coach others to carry on the mission. They share their knowledge and wisdom with others even if it means they may surpass them. They build a powerful network of teams who are committed to the vision. Even in their absence, their impact is strengthened. They promote and value teamwork. It's not a one-man sprint but a team marathon relay. The work must go even when you are not there anymore.

"The final test of a leader is that he leaves behind him in other men the conviction and the will to carry on." —Walter Lippmann

SECTION TWO

Leadership Styles for Building & Fostering Teamwork

CHAPTER SEVEN

INSPIRATIONAL LEADERSHIP

Keeping Hope Alive

"We have always held to the hope, the belief, the conviction, that there is a better life, a better world, beyond the horizon." —Franklin D. Roosevelt.

Given the current unstable environment, leaders need to inspire hopefulness in those around them. Thus organizations that want to instil a mind-set of hope among their workforce require trustworthiness and inspiration from those at the top. Hope is a fundamental aspect of the human condition as breath is to life. We all hope; maybe not for the same things, maybe not for the same reasons, maybe not with the same intensity—but we all, nonetheless, hope. A businessman, down and out in Paris, considered his options: among them, jumping off the Eiffel Tower. Life and business were going downhill. It could be over so soon. All his problems would be solved—on impact! Yet he hesitated and lingered, not so much out of fear of dying; he hesitated because, amidst all the hurt and despair, there was still a ray of hope that there might be a God who loves and cares about him. And it was this glimmer of hope that kept him from jumping.

German Philosopher Immanuel Kant boiled down life to three great questions: What can I know? What ought I do? What can I hope?

Today it seems that hope is in short supply. People are hope-starved. It is not difficult to understand why there has been a loss of hope in our society. Historians often try to label the various eras: the Age of Reason, the Age of Aquarius, the Lost Generation, the Modem Era, the Post Modern Era, and so forth. The labels only partially fit, because they describe only a part of the whole, rarely the whole itself. This era is being called the "Fourth Industrial

Revolution," and it is deeply altering the way we live, work and relate to one another. Every day we see the development of new technologies and the gap continues to widen between progress and society's ability to handle its consequences. We see the drastic shifts that occur as these technologies become engrained in our lives.

> "Hope is an orientation of the spirit, an orientation of the heart; it transcends the world that is immediately experienced, and is anchored somewhere beyond its horizons." —Vaclav Havel, former Czech Republic President

Most individuals have a desire for some level of certainty and assurance in their lives. Who would get on an aeroplane without some confidence, that it was well-maintained and mechanically sound or that the pilots were experienced? Who would join a company without some assurance that the organization would be around for some time? Who would go to the doctor without a belief in the practitioner's competency in medicine? All of us, in one way or another, look for and need a certain level of assurance in our everyday lives.

In 1516, Sir Thomas More wrote about a nation with little crime and no poverty. In this beautiful land, everyone had enough work; the sick were adequately taken care of, cities were well designed and wonderfully created, the people enjoyed complete religious liberty and the greatest pleasure for the inhabitants was obtained from doing good to others. The name of this land? *Utopia*

All around us, we see exploitation and a gradual descent toward dissolution. In fact, the second law of thermodynamics teaches, that every day the physical world around us is moving towards disintegration, chaos, and disorder. It is a natural law. Yet, there is always hope, in spite of whatever trials and struggles we may face.

Man," wrote Francisco José Moreno, "is afraid. Fear is one of the fundamental motivating forces behind our actions:

Fear of the past (your shortcomings will be found out).

Fear of the future (things may not get better).

Fear in the present (each day brings new trials).

Many definitions of hope contain the word *expectation*, the implication being towards the future. The very concept of hope implies something we do not yet have but expect or want to have. It is a future expectation and anticipation. Hope keeps us alive. It leads us to keep putting one foot in front the other. Hope is a primary motivator in a leader's life. Sometimes, the problems and troubles of life seem to be overwhelming. Today many people are facing fears over job security, financial instability, family crises, broken relationships, health scares and bereavement. To be human is, to some degree or another, to know sorrow and disappointment. There can be stormy nights without stars, long days without sunshine. The historian of antiquity Herodotus wrote about a culture in which people mourned—yes, wept when a baby was born, because they knew the inescapable sorrow and suffering that the child would face were he or she to reach adulthood. However, hope makes the real difference in life. Notwithstanding, you cannot take your hope and implant it into someone else. Hope has to be personally experienced, personally believed. However, you can encourage others and show them the great vision we are working towards that will bring a better future. Hope must be like an anchor: unchanging, enduring and stable. Hope motivates us to keep pursuing the mission.

If the past is a precursor to the future, all we can expect, to quote a former British politician, is blood, toil, tears, and sweat. Someone once said that at first, we hope too much and then, later, not enough. In our own experiences, this is often quite true. In our early years of leadership, hope can be so real and exciting. But, as time passes and with the ever increasing obstacles in our path, we begin to lose hope. Hope, stems from the idea that what's bad now will one day change; that what is causing us distress will be alleviated in the future. Hope points to something in the future that will cause us to be in a better place than what we are in now. Hope is not just some abstract concept. It is real and tangible.

Hope says, "No matter how tired, how discouraged, how sorrowful and sore you become, do not give up, do not stop trusting, do not stop believing, because the moment you do, everything you have done thus far will be in vain." Living the life of hope means making hope central. Hope gives meaning and purpose. It says where we are going and gives us the confidence to make a difference and help those around us. A trapeze performer was explaining how he accomplished a breath-taking triple somersault: "To catch the swing," he explained, "you must time your dive perfectly. It takes a lot of practice and courage. The secret is to throw your heart over the bar. And when you do that, your body will follow."

Giving hope to your people combines the alignment, engagement, and vision of the organization. Instilling hope in your team involves always looking at the bright side of things and taking the time to encourage them. In life, we all face different challenges. People want hope as it gives them something to look forward to; something to hold on to. Hope is being aware of what is going on with your employees and taking the time to connect with and inspire them. Hope has been proven to increase creativity, engagement and productivity, and that is what as leaders we aim for - To get the best out of our people who can positively affect the bottom line.

Cindy one of my former employees was close to retirement. She was going through a very tough time as she had lost her brother and father within a short space of time and her mother was very ill. I tried to help out as much as possible regarding granting her flex-time and authorizing her vacation schedule early on to deal with her personal responsibilities. She told me she wished she could retire sooner but could not afford to. Work became difficult for her as she was just going through the motions. She wanted to be home spending time with her ailing mother. Every time I passed by Cindy's desk, you could see the grief etched on her face. I would always tap her desk and tell her, "Come on Cindy cheer up! You will make it through. Just take it one day at a time. You can do this. Never lose hope!" I had the whole team pull together to always give little words of encouragement and drop small surprises on her desk to make her smile. Then the day came for Cindy to finally retire. I was sad to see her go but so happy for her. In her retirement speech, Cindy said, "Brigette I don't know what I would have done without you. You were the boss I needed at this very trying time in my life; so caring and understanding. You can't imagine the grief and pain I was going through, but you give me the support to make it through. You gave me hope."

3 Reasons to Practice Optimism in Leadership

"A pessimist sees the difficulty in every opportunity; an optimist the opportunity in every difficulty." —Winston Churchill

➢ Optimism is contagious. Researchers from Harvard University and the University of California in San Diego published their study on the subject of "emotional contagion" in 2008. The research stated that people who are surrounded by individuals who are happy will most likely become happier themselves. Additionally, Hay Group a global management consulting firm found that leaders' attitude and behaviour can have a 70% positive impact on organizational climate. Therefore a leader's outlook, whether negative or positive will spread. Being in a negative workplace can affect employees' commitment and subsequent productivity. This is why leaders should consider creating a positive working environment.

➢ Optimism brings creativity to problem-solving. Researchers Charles Carver and Michael Scheier studied the effects of optimism on results in their 1985 study, "Optimism, Coping, and Health: Assessment and Implications of Generalized Outcome Expectancies".   Michael Scheier said of their research results: "We know why optimists do better than pessimists. The answer lies in the differences between the coping strategies they use. Optimists are not simply being Pollyannas; they're problem solvers who try to improve the situation . . . Pessimists, on the other hand, tend to deny, avoid, and distort the problems they confront, and dwell on their negative feelings. It's easy to see now why pessimists don't do so well compared to optimists."

➢ Optimism promotes resiliency. Nobel Prize winning economist, Daniel Kahneman, discussed his research on optimists in his book, Thinking Fast and Slow. In it, he said it's the resilience of optimists their ability to acclimatize and rebound, that make them stand out from everybody else. "Their confidence in their future success sustains a positive mood that helps them obtain resources from others, raise the morale of their employees, and enhance their prospects of prevailing. When action is needed, optimism, even of the mildly delusional variety, may be a good thing."

Inspirational Leadership Theory

The Inspirational Leadership Theory model created by Dr. William Austin. He states an inspirational leader has an inspirational agenda to create a culture that educates, motivates, inspires, and supports followers. This theory combines management and leadership with the goal of empowering followers to become future leaders. It acts as a set of core qualities used to inspire an organization around an inspirational agenda (Austin, 2009). Research on inspirational leadership has shown links to an increase in follower engagement in organizations. It was also observed that inspirational leaders display specific characteristics that make that leader unique (McEarchern, 2005).

Bono and Ilies (2006) reported that a leader who is emotionally positive has the greatest chance of being perceived as effective. Shamir, House, and Arthur (1993) state that certain leader behaviours can have a profound impact on motivating followers. Particular leader behaviours trigger positive aspects of a follower's self-concept. This leads to follower motivation as well as new opportunities for future motivation. The inspiring leader is perceived by followers to be knowledgeable, enlightened and sensitive to the problems at hand (Bass, 1988). More importantly, inspirational leaders tend to have emotional intelligence which allows them to encourage extraordinary performance and greatness from their followers (Belsten, 2010).

McEarchern (2005) reports that inspirational leadership comes from a combination of emotional and spiritual intelligence. Emotional intelligence is the extent to which a leader is aware of the emotional environment of the organization and the emotional lives of followers. Spiritual intelligence is creating a sense of belief and purpose within an organization. These two broad concepts show up in Austin's model under what he labels "Arouse Feelings & Ideas" and "Envision a Spirit." Austin's ideal inspirational model begins to describe the interaction between leader, followers, and the surrounding culture emphasizing eight practices. **These eight practices are:**

➢ Create a quest for the "Holy Grail," – This challenges a leader to project a unique vision for the organization. Emphasized are shared personal and professional values and goals aligned with organizational goals. It means having a mission that represents a consensus of need and direction for the organization.

➢ Create a sense of urgency - The "status quo" is challenged by taking risks that could potentially lead to greater success. This is achieved by highlighting issues, communicating these matters, and empowering individuals to find solutions. It also includes identifying leaders as they emerge from followers, and empowering those new leaders to lead.

- Trust instincts over figures - An inspirational leader is confident in his/her preparation and allows instinct to guide decision-making. It is the ability of leaders to draw upon past life experience to help interpret data and make effective decisions. Through the leader's experience and instinct, followers will get a sense of how in touch with reality the leader is.

- Hold the line on integrity – This challenges a leader to create an organizational environment built on trust and integrity. This practice is described as a leader creating, promoting, and embodying integrity, trust and honesty in everything that is done personally and professionally. A common technique is to use teamwork and collaboration to foster relationships that develop individuals professionally and personally. Such leaders hold employees to high standards and don't accept anything less than that.

- Break the management rules: This includes eliminating bureaucratic processes by opening the lines of communication and giving employees more autonomy. The inspirational leader strives to be fair and is attentive to matching talent with the task. It also includes making an effort to move poor-performing employees into different positions that would allow opportunities for individual success and publicly rewarding star performers to inspire poor performing staff to work harder. The inspirational leader openly praises and rewards members for the achievement of goals, thus promoting a culture of risk, creativity and transparency.

- Believe in your people - Leaders believe in their followers' abilities to be leaders and learners. This highlights the importance of trust and responsibility between the leader and the team. The inspirational leader recognizes that followers do not need to be micromanaged to perform their work. They set high expectations for employees, give them autonomy in their positions, and support failures as opportunities to learn.

➢ Demonstrate through results - This practice is described as a leader following through on initiatives, goals, and commitments. The inspirational leader only accepts reward and praise when it is earned or once the activity is completed.

➢ Share the wealth. The inspirational leader promotes altruism and a commitment to the organization's goals. The inspirational leader will reward followers before accepting reward or praise for themselves. The result is that followers are inspired to work harder by their free will and not just because of the reward.

10 Steps To Be More Inspirational:

The dictionary definition of inspirational is "to fill (someone) with the urge or ability feel or do something especially creative." Inspirational leaders capture heart, mind and spirit of their team and find joy in doing so. Research has shown that inspiring work environment increases 40% employee engagement, 40% gain in customer satisfaction and 35% gain in profits. A study conducted by the Center for Creative Leadership called The Challenges Leaders Face Around the World: More similar than different. It reveals that inspiring others is one of the six top challenges leaders struggle with. Today's workplaces, organized with technology and virtual workers scattered far apart, are requiring a new set of guidelines for inspirational leadership. Command and control styles are giving way to new purpose-driven leaders who seek to capture the hearts and loyalties of workers.

1 Model the performance you seek. **Lead by example—Show** employees what behaviours you expect. Don't expect others to perform actions that you are not demonstrating. Action is everything. Treat everyone you come in contact with respect and compassion. Be approachable. Make it possible for others to feel comfortable to come to you to discuss ideas or problems.

2 Share the Right Values. **Inspirational Leaders are viewed as** honest and trustworthy. In 2005, Scott Lichtenstein, in a research paper called Values, Observable Characteristics, Strategic Choice and Behavior and Performance Elements of the Upper Echelon Theory, revealed that a leader's values had a direct impact on their organization's performance. Ultimately, inspiring leadership is about trust. Organizations need to stand for something, not just exist for their own ends, and inspirational leaders are about spreading the right values that drive the organization to achieve excellent results. "My experience is that significant distrust doubles the cost of doing business and triples the time it takes to get things done. Trust is like a performance multiplier, enabling organisations to succeed in their communications, interactions, and decisions, and to move with incredible speed.

A recent Watson Wyatt study showed that high trust companies outperform low trust companies by nearly 300%! " —Stephen Covey

3 Be Authentic. The concept of authenticity means many different things to different people. It basically is not putting on a show and being true to yourself. Be, genuine, humble and real. If you try to be something you're not, others will know it and so will you; you can't fake it for too long. Some leaders may pull it off for a while, but eventually, the truth comes to light. Who you really are is embedded naturally within you. Lack of authenticity is revealed in both body language and impromptu comments in unguarded moments. Authenticity builds trust. Inspirational leaders are authentic. They genuinely care about people and empower people to lead. If you pretend to care about other people, they won't respond much to your interest. If you actually care, they will open up to you.

4 Show unwavering Integrity and Accountability; always do the right thing. A true leader is open, honest and delivers results. Trust can be developed and improved. And it needs to be maintained. According to the 2011 HOW Report, only 9 percent of employees work in high-trust organizations.

5 Be Optimistic and Positive - Hone your ability to inspire and motivate others. A naturally positive leader will have a passion for their work and inspire those around them. Fill yourself with positive energy so you can shower it on your people and all those you meet. They will feel it, and they will want more, from seeing the inspiration you exude. Your voice, speech, and body language will inspire commitment in the chosen direction. Motivate your team to give their best by expressing your passion, communicating with optimism, and connecting tasks to a greater purpose. Inspire them to act by continuously engaging

their talents, re-recruiting their spirit, and celebrating successes. Work on building the resilient mind-set and capabilities for your organization to survive and prosper in these challenging times.

6 | Be Fully Human - Do not be afraid to show some vulnerability. Vulnerability shared honestly is powerful. Develop strong communications through compelling storytelling and active listening. Use storytelling to show your humanity, revealing both your successes and failures. Such leaders seek honest feedback about themselves and their leadership. They honour others openly. They sincerely empathize with others. By showing empathy, leaders can see the world through another's eyes.

7 | Demonstrate Courage - Great leaders will have the courage of their convictions and the willpower to see it through. Nelson Mandela dared to fight against the structure of apartheid. Even when faced with 20 years in prison, he still held onto his beliefs of right and wrong. Mahatma Gandhi was the political leader of India during the Indian independence movement. Despite being detained numerous times, his determination continued until independence was duly granted. When you demonstrate courage, people will respect you and want to follow you.

8 | Build relationships - cultivate heart-centred communication and connect with others. Have confidence and trust in your employees which gives them real empowerment. Cultivate your self-awareness and be awake to the present moment. Be interested in your team. Practice deep listening more than talking. There is nothing more powerful than witnessing a leader who genuinely engages with their team.

9 | Offer feedback that emphasizes the positive. Focus on developing your people. The way you offer feedback can be immensely inspirational. Your team wants to know if they are performing up

to expectations. Structure your feedback in a way that focuses on their strengths and which shows your belief in their capacity for growth and improvement.

10 Be generous with praise and rewards. Acknowledge your team for a job well done and follow this up with meaningful rewards. Celebrate every success. Even if it seems small, still celebrate the little milestones. Show appreciation and celebrate the contributions made by your team. It will inspire them to give more.

Inspirational Leadership foster Teamwork. Creating and maintaining a positive organizational climate helps to improve team dynamics. Team dynamics are created by the individuals on the team, their personalities, working relationships with one another and the environment in which the team works. Great leaders demonstrate the ability not only to build great teams but also to get the very best out of them. Sir Ernest Shackleton was the principal figure of the period known as the Heroic Age of Antarctic Exploration. In 1914, he led an ill-fated expedition to cross the Antarctica via the South

Pole, but the expedition was cut short when their ship became stuck in ice. Despite being trapped for nearly two years, Shackleton's inspirational leadership was essential in forming and nurturing a competent team to handle each and every challenge along the way. Astonishingly, not a single member of his 28-men team died during the nearly two years they were stranded. Just as the carpenter is always near his timber, the potter is always close to his clay, and the blacksmith is not far from his metal, so also the Leader is always there to inspire us.

> "Leadership is lifting a person's vision to high sights, the raising of a person's performance to a higher standard, the building of a personality beyond its normal limitations". — Peter Drucker

When we inspire people, they are more engaged and motivated to excel in their personal and professional lives. Inspirational leaders leave legacies that long exceed their time at the reins of the companies they have served.

CHAPTER EIGHT

SERVANT LEADERSHIP

The traditional top – down, command and control management *style,* where managers issue orders and employees must comply or disciplinary action is applied, doesn't work anymore. Today that style practised exclusively is ineffective. Followers expect more and demand more from leaders. Leadership is a privilege. Robert Greenleaf first coined Servant Leadership in his essay. "The Servant as Leader"(1970), (Even though the concept existed thousands of years ago, the perfect example being Jesus Christ Himself). In that essay, Greenleaf wrote: "The servant-leader is servant first... It begins with the natural feeling that one wants to serve, to serve first. Then conscious choice brings one to aspire to lead. That person is sharply different from one who is leader first, perhaps because of the need to assuage an unusual power drive or to acquire material possessions...The leader-first and the servant-first are two extreme types. Between them, there are shadings and blends that are part of the infinite variety of human nature.' Greenleaf also stated that "The difference manifests itself in the care taken by the servant-first to make sure that other people's highest priority needs are being served. The best test, and difficult to administer, is: Do those served grow as persons? Do they, while being served, become healthier, wiser, freer, more autonomous, more likely themselves to become servants? And, what is the effect on the least privileged in society? Will they benefit or at least not be further deprived?"

Servant Leadership is a philosophy in which the leader places emphasis on the needs of the follower over the self-interests of the leader. It involves the ability of the leader to demonstrate characteristics of stewardship and a commitment to personal growth toward others. To be a servant leader, a heart for service has to be embedded in your core values. When a leader seeks to be self-serving rather than a servant of the people, he opens up himself to error. Leaders are only as successful as the quality of the teams they have created and led. Sustainable enterprise success requires a balance of competitive and cooperative approaches. Good leaders do not use power for self-empowerment; they use it to empower those around them. Servant leadership is powerful, practical, and personal.

According to research published in the Academy of Management Journal, employees feel the most valued and, in return, give back to the organization and its customers when their leaders create a culture of fairness, trust, cooperation and empathy. As stated by Sandy Wayne, one of the authors of the research: "The best business leadership style is far from, 'Do this. Don't do that'. A *servant leader* looks and sounds a lot more like, 'Is there anything I can do to help you?' or 'Let me help you...' or 'What do you need to...?' This approach helps employees reach their full potential." The corresponding appreciation employees have for their leaders who genuinely care about them manifests itself in teamwork and commitment to the company and its customers. "It's contagious," Wayne said. "The employees see their leaders as role models and often mimic those qualities, creating a culture of servant leadership. This serving culture drives the effectiveness of the business as a whole."

> "The rare individuals who unselfishly try to serve others have an enormous advantage - have little competition." — Andrew Carnegie

As a materialistic society, we have fixed metrics for success that is based on external indicators. When our value as a leader is evaluated by our "doing" metrics rather than from our inner self, it shifts us to focus on self. From a practical standpoint, moving from a numbers driven mentality to one which fosters internal growth is not easy. Balancing the needs of your team with your own needs will give you the best chance at accomplishing both your teams' goals and your own. Jim Heskett, in a 2013 post for Harvard Business Review, asked why servant leadership was not more widespread. His readers seemed to agree that, "most people are too selfish or too concerned with getting credit to be servant-leaders."

"I have found the concept of servant leadership to be an effective way of communicating with and motivating today's employees. It simply entails being a support mechanism for them...the mind-set of "what can I do to make your job easier"... that allows them to do their jobs better and more effectively. It creates a culture of empowerment that allows people to take ownership of their duties and find more satisfaction that they make a difference in the company's performance." —Stephen J. Wildman, President and Owner of Advanced Staging Productions,

Leaders should possess the manner of a humble and selfless servant (Spears, 1994) to inspire and influence their team. Get out of your comfort zone and interact with your people. Servant leaders are not afraid to get their hands dirty as they value the input of team members. They don't ask others to do what they wouldn't be willing to do themselves. They show employees how things are done. You must be "present" to guide employees throughout the process and facilitate the teams' ability to create "plans of action". Actions do speak louder than words; especially your actions. Words in the air, they say, is just vapour. Actions reflect the truth, and they create teachable moments for future leaders. To be a servant leader is to be more accessible than ever. Everyone knows they can come to you without feeling intimidated or facing rejection. Such leaders "walk the talk." They remove the hierarchical barriers. I always tell my employees, my door is open if there is anything they need to see me about urgently; whether personal or professional, don't hesitate to knock. The result is that it has strengthened my relationship with my team. They know I am always here for them and when I need something done immediately or require they come in the office earlier to ensure we don't miss a deadline; they make the extra effort and give me the support I need. Leadership thrives on both a "give and take' philosophy. *You cannot achieve success without your team, so it pays to invest time in them.* I am aware that my responsibility as company Director lies in my staff being proud to work for me. Daily I remind myself how privileged I am to serve these amazing and competent people. As a leader, it is easy to get wrapped up in the "things" however; great results are achieved when you are connected with your employees, leading by example, mentoring and promoting an atmosphere of teamwork. That is when a group of people become a TEAM—cohesive and synergistic, simply because employees are engaged and empowered to do the right thing.

"Setting an example is not the main means of influencing another, it is the only means." —Albert Einstein

10 Qualities of Servant Leaders

1 **Self-Awareness and Emotional Intelligence:** Self-awareness is the skill of recognizing and understanding your emotions, motivations and thoughts. It is the capacity for introspection and the ability to know your psychological state. It is having a clear picture of your strengths and weaknesses. Knowing your areas of weakness allows you to delegate to others who are proficient in those abilities, in order to achieve the common goal. Great leaders are aware of their limits, so they surround themselves with individuals who complement, rather than supplement, their skills. Working on your areas of weaknesses will improve your leadership ability. Self-awareness is the foundation of Emotional Intelligence. Emotional Intelligence (EI or EQ – Emotional Quotient) is a modern concept that was popularized by Daniel Goleman. Emotional intelligence by definition is the capability of individuals to recognize their own and other

179

people's emotions; to distinguish between different feelings and label them appropriately, to use emotional information to guide thinking and behaviour, and to control and adjust emotions to achieve one's goals. It involves:

❖ Self-Awareness—the ability to recognize one's emotions and internal states.

❖ Self-Management—capacity to manage one's emotions and adapt to changing circumstances.

❖ Social Awareness—the ability to discern, understand and react to others' feelings, needs and concerns while comprehending social networks.

❖ Relationship Management—the ability to inspire, influence and develop others while managing conflict.

Leaders with high emotional intelligence know what they're feeling and how these emotions can affect other people. It involves constant reflection. Leaders must have a firm understanding of how their emotions and actions affect the people around them. Servant leaders possess high emotional intelligence. Research shows that leaders with high emotional intelligence find it easier to form and maintain interpersonal relationships and perform better than leaders who lack this skill. *Empathy is* a hallmark trait of those with high *emotional intelligence. It's t*he ability to understand and share the feelings of another and is essential in a servant leadership culture. You place yourself in the individual's shoes; experiencing emotions that match another person's emotions and discerning what another person is thinking or feeling. You should always pay attention to your body language. Make sure your body language emphasizes the message you're giving. Empathy helps us to develop a stronger understanding of other people's situations. It includes having a service orientation towards people. This can only make for better and more impactful decision-making as you take a 360-degree view of situations. Leading with empathy and serving others and empowering them is the guide for excellent leadership. Servant leaders build relationships, not power structures that allow people to work together to meet the challenges of an ever-changing industry landscape. They prioritize the practice of presence. They give people their full attention so they can be fully present in the moment rather than distracted by multi-tasking. There is strength in servant leadership; servant leadership does not mean one is weak on the contrary, you have to be strong to serve in the first place. You must be willing to share your gifts, inspire and develop others rather than being someone who is power-driven that takes all the credit. It's not micromanaging because that builds distrust, it's not being intimidated by a high flyer on your team. Servant leaders often have a quiet confidence and an abundance of belief in themselves and those they lead and serve.

"We make a living by what we get. We make a life by what we give."—Winston Churchill

2 | Patience: In Greek, two words express the meaning of patience; the first is hupomone, translated "endurance, steadfastness, and fortitude" in circumstances that cannot be changed. The second word, makrothumia, means "great" or "long tempered." It is the opposite of short-tempered, impatient, and easily frustrated. It means putting up with others or with situations even when things do not run smoothly. A patient person is composed, and constant. Patience does not come naturally. It is something we must cultivate especially in this digital era. The real test of patience is not in the waiting but in how one behaves while waiting. Life is full of waiting. We may be waiting on a deal to

close, a merger to be finalized or new employees to come up to speed. We are normally impatient about things that we really want or have been promised but don't have yet. We are often satisfied only when we get what we are yearning for. And if we don't get what we want when we want it, it means that we are often doomed to frustration and impatience. And when we are in this state, it is almost impossible to maintain an inner peace. Learning patience is not easy. An organization is composed of diverse individuals from various backgrounds and cultures. It also includes people who are on different rungs of the maturity ladder. Patience is necessary to be able to get along with others especially when there are so many differences. It can be easy for those who are experienced and proficient to be impatient towards those who aren't. Is there a point where our patience can justifiably run out when dealing with people in a difficult situation? It depends on what the underlying circumstances are. We might decide that we've had enough of a particular situation and decide that it has to end. But that's not the same thing as being judgmental or cruel in the process. The time might come to take action, but that action must never be out of agreement with the principles of respect and empathy. When we have patience, it will be easy for us to train, coach and teach others and this is what great leaders do. They are great teachers. They pass on their knowledge and wisdom to others. They are interested in the growth of their team and in making more leaders.

3 | **Humility.** Being genuine and humble are some of the qualities servant leaders possess. "The first responsibility of a leader is to define reality. The last is to say thank you. In between, the leader is a servant." —Max de Pree. Servant Leaders are open to feedback and don't take things personally even if they are unfairly treated. They lead with vulnerability and are not afraid to say "I don't know." Invite Participation: Using this technique will help you create a culture of trust, and share power. Humility should

wash away from our hearts any residue of arrogance and sense of superiority. Servant Leaders are great listeners—quick to listen and slow to speak. They listen with the intent of understanding. They respect those they work with. It's important to always check on your Speaking—Listening ratio when interacting with others. Servant leaders influence others based on building trust and respectful relationships. The servant leader is one that also knows when to be quiet. When we are still, we see and hear things that may easily be missed. If you want to know the bright ideas of the people on your team and get to the root cause of problems to better solve problems, you need to listen. "A true natural servant automatically responds to any problem by listening first." — Robert Greenleaf. The capacity to listen is much as important as the capacity to speak your thoughts. A young man asked Socrates to teach him oratory. Because he talked so much, Socrates asked for double fees. "Why are you charging me double?" the young student asked. "Because I must teach you two sciences: the one, how to hold your tongue, and the other, how to speak.

4 | **Authenticity and Integrity.** Servant Leaders are transparent and walk with integrity. Such individuals possess a high level of self-awareness. They are honest with employees about what is going on. Tony Simons' Integrity Dividend offers more proof. His research teams found that leaders who demonstrate behavioural integrity; keep their promises and live their organization's values and inspire employees to serve customers better and earn greater profits. We are selected because the people believe that we will do great things and make them better off. Servant leadership is authentic and will have a long-lasting effect on any organization. To be a "Servant Leader" necessitates a modification of attitude and inner transformation, not a set of skills (Wong & Davey, 2007). Every leader should have someone to whom he or she is accountable, and that requires humility. When leaders focus on external indulgence instead of internal growth, they lose their

way. Often they reject the realist who speaks truth. Instead, they surround themselves with sycophants who stroke their egos. Eventually, they openly refuse to engage in honest dialogue and others learn not to confront them with reality. To be a servant leader is basically to undress vanity and ego. Leaders need to stay in touch with the right people - people who will be honest with you. This is especially needed the higher up the corporate ladder you go. Leaders are expected to demonstrate certain values which society demands from a leader. These values help the leader to make principled decisions. A leader is the sum total of their values, which followers try to emulate to become like them. Servant leaders do right by their people, and their people do right by the company. People are counting on you to do what is correct. Be truthful, honest and trustworthy. People crave consistency. When what's agreed upon is consistently delivered by a leader then trust and respect are built, and relationships are strengthened.

5 | **A genuine passion for people.** Servant leadership is a people-centred approach to life and leadership, which puts other people at the centre. It places the needs, and growth and development of those being led, ahead of those leading. They focus on and invest time in people. Be "in the moment", observe, provide constructive feedback and say "thank you" often. We all make mistakes. To grow, we require valuable feedback along the way. I make time to have one to one conversations with my team to show them my support and care. Building their talent is a top priority. They have a concern for everyone who interacts with the business. Servant leaders understand that everyone wants to be encouraged at an individual level. Servant leaders focus on serving others rather than gaining fame, affluence, and power for themselves. Serving the needs of others should always be at the forefront of any company. We live in a society where there seems to be less kindness and more indifference, aggressiveness and impoliteness. Sometimes it comes as a pleasant surprise to others when we treat them with gentleness. Our world needs more kindness. Wherever we live, we see many people around us with sad faces, who have given up. They do not really live. Nothing cost so little and goes so far as courtesy yet it seems to be rare. Kindness is being respectful, not looking down on others. It is being exemplary and not domineering. It is embracing equality and refuting superiority. Often patience might be manifested by doing nothing, however kindness, in contrast, is manifested by what we say and do and, most importantly, by how we say it and do it. **Kindness** is not beyond the reach of any leader, although it may require the sacrifice of time and energy. Kindness is a verb that reveals itself in various ways. And like its sister "love," kindness contains incredible power. Kindness, especially in our organizations, is crucial. It's putting people before technology and listening with constant empathy. And one of the most important ways we can manifest kindness is

in the way we speak to each other. The atmosphere of the organization is largely determined by the words we speak. So many problems, so many hurts, and outright conflicts could be avoided if we were both careful with what we say and how we say it. At times one could say something to someone and not offend or hurt them, and another time the same words one would say to the same person would greatly hurt them. Speech is more than just the meanings of words themselves; it's tone, facial expression and body language.

So often, how we treat others comes back on ourselves. In general, how we treat others will impact how we are treated. If we are kind, it's more likely that others will be kind to us. It works the other way around as well: be mean to others, and they usually will reciprocate the same behaviour towards you. Of course, it doesn't always happen that way. But whether it does or doesn't, in one sense it doesn't really matter. As leaders, we always should be kind, even if that kindness is not returned to us. In fact, being kind to those who are unkind to us is a hallmark of being a true leader. Therefore, "do unto others as you would have them do unto you." It's always easy to be kind to someone who could be of benefit to you now or later down the road. Anyone can do that. What's difficult, is to be kind, to those who can never do anything for you in return, especially when it costs you something. That's the real test. Alexander Maclaren, a well-known London clergyman of the late nineteenth century, wrote: "Gentleness is the strongest force in the world. You take all the steam hammers that were ever forged and battle at an iceberg, and except for the comparatively little heat that is developed by the blows and melts some small portion, it will still be ice, though pulverized instead of whole. But let it move gently down to the southward, there the sunbeams smite the coldness of death, and it is dissipated in the warm ocean. Kindness is conquering."

6 **Pursue Succession planning:** Do those being served grow as people? Servant-Leaders share information & power; help others in any way they can, and give of their time and resources. They trust their teams thus providing access to information whereby empowering them with the resources necessary to make wise decisions. They show employees that they believe in them. Their selfless example of leadership builds teams of individuals who also want to be of service to others. When putting their legitimate wants aside and fighting for their follower's right, then leaders will gain more trust (Spears & Lawrence, 2004). Such leaders are generous with their time and resources and are focused on supporting, and developing the people on their teams. They are interested in *m*aking more leaders rather than just having more followers. The servant leader directs, guides and provides inspiration to help motivate people. They create a positive workplace environment; members know exactly what's expected of them, and they understand the strategy of the company. The servant leader develops people for the future.

7 **Accountability** - A man sued a fast-food company, claiming that his obesity, and the subsequent health problems that followed from it, resulted from him eating five meals a week at the fast-food restaurant. He blamed the company, not himself, for his problems. We can sometimes be like that, blaming others for our misdeeds. Human nature is always looking for someone else to blame for its problems, always looking for an excuse not to take responsibility for one's actions. In 2016, Wells Fargo was fined $185 million for illegal sales tactics practices that included employees opening as many as two million accounts for customers without their knowledge. We saw a lack of accountability during this crisis when then-CEO John Stumpf attempted to do everything in his power to manage this shattering crisis in a way that allowed him to keep his job. However, it didn't work as he was forced to retire to be replaced by Tim Sloan as CEO. We do not live the leadership life in isolation, but in a community. As leaders, we should be held accountable for the impact our negative actions have on others livelihood. Leaders who value trustworthiness hold themselves responsible for the decisions they have made and accept the consequences of their actions.

8 **Continuous Learning:** Today's business leaders know to achieve success, they must commit to lifelong learning. Servant-Leaders invest in the development of themselves and in their people. They discover the aspirations of the people on their team and

look for opportunities to help them grow. They see potential in people and keep inspiring them to reach their full potential. A servant leader grows by helping his followers to grow. They encourage the personal and professional growth of all individuals in the capacity of a teacher. They are forgiving and look beyond employees' faults and push them to strengthen their weaker areas and develop strengths. This reinforcement to forgive is essential in the creation of a culture where it is accepted that people will and do make mistakes. Failure doesn't keep such leaders down; they push everyone to keep moving forward to brighter and better days ahead. They know that people can achieve amazing things when they are inspired by a purpose beyond themselves. They have a great vision for themselves, their team and of the future of the organization.

9 **Social Responsibility**—Servant Leaders put employees and those in their community first. These leaders place themselves where they can influence by doing good for those they lead and by giving their team something to believe in. They promote a culture of giving back. "The purpose of life is not to win. The purpose of life is to grow and to share. When you come to look back on all that you have done in life, you will get more satisfaction from the pleasure you have brought into other people's lives than you will from the times that you outdid and defeated them" —Rabbi Harold Kushner. David W. Ballard, PsyD, MBA, head of APA's Psychologically Healthy Workplace Program stated: "Successful organizations have learned that high performance and sustainable results require attention to the relationships among employee, organization, customer and community."

10 **Reward and Recognition.** Servant leaders *give* credit where it is due. They prefer to let others have the spotlight. They accept responsibility when failure happens. They don't throw a team member *under the bus* to make themselves look good when

189

something goes wrong. They are always on the lookout for required behaviours. It's important to encourage people when you see them doing something right– Sure it's important to give feedback when people do something wrong, but it's even more important when you see them doing something right. Reinforcing feedback makes people feel great and encourages people to do more of the same. Openly acknowledging and rewarding the contributions of others inspires and ignites passion which translates into increased productivity. "Thank you" is a frequent word in the vocabulary of the servant leader. "You need to be aware of what others are doing, applaud their efforts, acknowledge their successes, and encourage them in their pursuits. When we all help one another, everybody wins."
—Jim Stovall

Servant Leadership Promotes Teamwork

Grounded in cooperation and egalitarianism, the servant leader involves followers in decision making. Rather than taking arbitrary decisions, such leaders seek to include the people in the process. The servant leader works in close collaboration with team members, focusing on building relationships and rapport. They show respect for everyone. Acceptance of the individuality of all employees provides the foundation for stimulating the unique ideas and perspectives of employees and additionally assures them that they matter in the organisation. A genuine appreciation and respect for everyone's contribution and their roles is essential to building trust. The servant leader is effective at building consensus within groups as they primarily rely on persuasion rather than positional power. Servant leaders are flexible and give their team autonomy. Team members tend to have high job satisfaction and are productive because they're more involved in decisions. They focus on more WE and less ME. "The leaders who work most effectively, scarcely say "I." And that is because they think, "we"; they think "team." They understand their job is to make the team function effectively. They accept responsibility and don't sidestep because it is "we" that gets the credit. This is what builds trust and enables you to get tasks completed.

Making it your primary role to serve others is both satisfying and rewarding. It builds strong relationships, sets an inspiring example and develops more servant leaders. Many leaders are obsessed with all sorts of prestige to place themselves in a spotlight. Becoming a servant leader shows strength of character. Humility is the inward adorning, the ornament of meekness adorns the inner self. This attribute is often the result of having developed a highly moral and spiritual character. Mastering servant leadership increases your influence and it is a lifelong learning process. Demanding and controlling managers, reduce employee morale and break team spirit which results in decreased employee engagement. However, some situations call for leaders to apply directive control over their team as; the amount of time available to accomplish a task, resistance showed by team members, the complexity of the task and the level of risk involved. Wise leaders will know how and when to switch between the servant leadership and autocratic style effectively. Leaders unavoidably must make tough decisions. But servant leaders balance authority and unlock immense influence by uniting heart, head, and hands in service to others.

Conclusion

When I truly embrace the above behaviours, I am a servant leader. I am serving, I am coaching, I am empowering, and I am lifting my team up to achieve their full potential. If all leaders follow the servant leadership, how different human history could have been! Sadly, leaders who are willing to serve are few and far between. But being a servant leader is a passion and an investment that always yields invaluable returns!

CHAPTER NINE

TRANSFORMATIONAL LEADERSHIP

In today's fast-paced, digital world, many employees are connected by technology and not physical proximity which was the norm a couple of years ago. Organizations are operating in an increasingly dynamic environment. Over the last century, the world has gone from being a national, resource-based economy to a more global, knowledge-based one. The opening up of international markets and the move towards a more 'Global' economy has intensified competition. Organizations have gone from gradually evolving to significantly transforming in response to the changing external environment. Companies are adopting downsizing and restructuring. These measures have taken a toll on workers and broke the traditional social contract of long-term employment in return for employee commitment. This has created internal complexities that require a leadership style which is adaptable and can also motivate staff. Transformational leadership is, therefore, well-suited to these current times which is characterized by organizational instability and global turbulence. Leaders need to master this style of leadership which calls for personal as well as team development. The transformational leadership style is also associated with charismatic and visionary leadership as it combines a bit of both. Transformational leaders need charisma and vision. Charisma relies on the charm and persuasiveness of the leader to encourage certain behaviours in followers. All great leaders are visionaries. They see into the future and turn that vision into reality.

Transactional Leadership

Transactional leadership focuses on the way leaders set tasks for followers. They assign tasks, manage those tasks, and give out rewards as they see fit. Additionally, employees who fail to achieve targets are disciplined. This type of leadership model is only successful when followers are completely devoted. It begins to fail when leaders abuse the contractual relationship by being unfair. Transactional leadership is the basis for hierarchical organizations where there is a clearly defined top and bottom layer with managers making up the middle. In today's globally competitive environment this transactional approach could be seen as being limited as Tichy & Devenna (1986, The transformational leader. Training and Development Journal, 40 (7) pp. 27-32) suggest: "Transactional leaders were fine for an era of expanding markets and non-existent competition. In return for compliance, they issued rewards. These managers changed little."

Transformation Leadership

Transformational leaders, in contrast, are attuned to the motives of followers and seek to win them over by appealing to their higher needs, including helping those less fortunate. Transformational leadership is strongly connected to the process of addressing the needs of followers so that the process of interaction increases the motivation and energy of others (Bass 1990). James MacGregor Burns first used the term transformational leadership in 1978 to describe a process in which "leaders and followers help each other to advance to a higher level of morale and motivation." Burns differentiated between transactional leaders, who exchanged tangible rewards for the commitment of followers, and transformational leaders who focused on higher order intrinsic needs. The idea of transformational leadership was further developed by Bernard Bass. Transformational leadership tends to be democratic, team oriented, human centred, and values based (Bass, 2008). By engaging followers on a humanistic level, a leader can gain personal trust in order to make a comprehensive change in the culture or value set of an organization (Burns, 1985). Building programs and processes that encourage proactive, collaborative, data-driven, and creative problem solving throughout the organization combined with a reflective learning component are fundamental to transformational leaders and organizations (Bass, 2008).

Transformational leadership is that which:

... facilitates a redefinition of a people's mission and vision, a renewal of their commitment and the restructuring of their systems for goal accomplishment. It is a relationship of mutual stimulation and elevation that converts followers into leaders and may convert leaders into moral agents. Hence, transformational leadership must be grounded in moral foundations.

(Leithwood, as cited in Cashin et al., 2000)

In 1985 Bernard Bass developed the Multifactor Leadership Questionnaire (MLQ), a tool intended to measure transactional and transformational leader behaviours. Following research studies involving commercial, military and educational organizations the MLQ has become the primary means of quantitatively assessing transformational leadership.

Transformational Leadership Theory has identified Four Leadership Competencies:

1 Individualized consideration: This can be seen in leaders paying close attention to individual employees' needs and motivations rather than treating everyone the same. Individualized consideration requires developing emotional intelligence and being a great listener. The leader by recognizing follower capabilities encourages the development of competences by setting an example and also through the delegation of challenging tasks. Such behaviours also cultivate organizational cultures that encourage personal development which is desirable in a highly competitive environment. Individual consideration is also achieved through expressing words of thanks or praise and fair workload distributions. The advantage of individualized attention could be seen in the context of globalization. The way in which successful organizations are restructuring and moving towards networked global firms has brought the realization that employees are a means of leveraging business success through diverse work teams.

2 Intellectual stimulation involves arousing and changing followers' awareness of problems and their capacity to solve those problems (Bono & Judge, 2004; Kelly, 2003). It includes motivating followers to engage in creative, and innovative thought through encouraging employees to evaluate old and current ways of thinking. A common misinterpretation is that transformational leaders are easygoing, but the fact is they constantly challenge followers to achieve higher levels of performance. Transformational leaders push present limits, raise the bar, stretch others beyond comfort zones, and challenge the status quo. Organizations that are continually growing & transforming need continuous productive disruption. They empower followers by persuading them to propose new and controversial ideas without fear of punishment or ridicule (Stone, Russell & Patterson, 200). There must be accountability. Hold everyone, including yourself, accountable. Share risk-taking – if something fails; own it, don't pinpoint and blame. Use mistakes as learning opportunities and do not criticize others. Give constructive feedback that will guide personal growth. Show you value independent thinking and reward people who challenge you.

3 Inspirational motivation is the quality that inspires and motivates employees to achieve higher performance levels. Transformational leaders inspire followers to become part of the overall organizational culture. It involves articulating a vision and mission, demonstrating interest and engaging with followers and the celebrating success. This can be achieved through motivational speeches and conversations in meetings and workshops. Provide two-way communication as feedback from the team is essential. Be direct and honest in your communications. Showing trust in the abilities of your team by giving them autonomy will help to motivate them. The leader encourages employees to look at the big picture and to aspire

to work towards something greater than themselves. Through this, long-term team performance is increased. The motivating effect of this form of leadership can also be felt in non-face-to-face contact as in virtual and geographically distant teams. The importance of motivation was demonstrated in an article by Jordan-Evans & Kaye (2002 Retaining Employees. Business: The Ultimate Resource, Bloomsbury Publishing, London, pp. 196-197) where they describe how employee talent may become the only distinguishing factor between a business and its competitors. They infer that there will be a global shortage in talent within the next 15 years and that retention of these highly skilled employees will be a significant challenge.

4 | Idealized Influence is about building confidence and trust. The leader serves as an ideal role model for followers; he/she demonstrates integrity as they 'walk the talk.' The concept of Idealized Influence is based on the idea that once the other three I's are fulfilled the followers will seek to emulate the behaviours of the leader and be willing to follow him\her. The confidence built and trust earned leads to commitment and loyalty of followers. Within this framework, this positive influence by a leader can make the difference between success and failure. This implication of idealized influence is also highlighted in an article by Odom & Green (2003, Law and the ethics of transformational leadership. Leadership & Organizational Development Journal, 24 (2) pp. 62-69). In this article, they discuss how organizations such as Enron facilitated unethical conduct which ultimately ended in their downfall. They suggest that transformational leadership would have helped to prevent such an event from happening due to the leaders focus on moral development and not just on the bottom line. The example set by leaders will eventually influence the culture and behaviours of individuals in the organization.

Individualized Consideration + Intellectual Stimulation + Inspirational Motivation + Idealized Influence = Exceed Expectations Performance

Seven Steps to becoming a Transformational Leader:

1 **Visionary**: Be a role model. Being a visionary is about setting a realistic vision that will paint a clear and compelling picture of the future. Transformational leaders mobilize everyone to get on board by passionately and articulately emphasizing the direction they want the company to pursue. They gave purpose. They practice optimism and express confidence in followers. They keep everyone focused on the big picture. Such leaders communicate, formally and informally, what they want to achieve in the world and others become connected to this leader in a personal way and to his or her vision. Followers are motivated to take action to achieve the leader's goals.

2 **Inspiration**: People want to be inspired. See the best in them and ignite them to reach for the stars. Inspire by the example you set in your words and actions. Transformational leaders have the ability to make those around them rise to the occasion. Inspiration comes by treating people as individuals and taking the time to understand what motivates them. According to Bass (1990) transformational leadership "occurs when leaders broaden and elevate the interests of their employees, when they generate awareness and acceptance of the purposes and mission of the group, and when they stir employees to look beyond their own self-interest for the good of the group."

3 **Value Driven** – Be known as a person of integrity. Employees will see you as a trustworthy person which will strengthen your ability

to influence them. Transformational leadership is tempered by introspection and reflection to ensure values and beliefs are guiding decisions. Such leaders have core values which they match with the corresponding behaviour. Confidence in leaders provides a foundation for employees to accept organizational change.

4 **Engage**: The transformational leader is one who values relationships. They are considerate about the personal needs of employees. He or she is authentic and connects with others by making the time to interact on a personal level. They adapt their leadership style to the different personalities and needs of their team. The transformational leader is interested in their people. Show that you care by demonstrating compassion and understanding. They lead changes through a shared vision and purpose, with an emphasis on relationship building.

5 **Employee Empowerment** – Encourage participation by removing barriers and give employees the necessary support and resources. Create the right conditions and frameworks for your team to effectively and efficiently complete tasks. Research has shown that employees who are empowered to participate not only in the decision-making process but who share a sense of ownership for what they do, provide better customer service. They are pro-active problem solvers who see their jobs as more than just their day to day tasks and get excited about how to add value. "Leaders must avoid the urge to answer every question or provide a solution to every problem. Instead, you must start asking the questions, seeing others as a source of innovation, and transferring ownership of the organizations growth. The greatest impact is that it unleashes the power of the many and loosens the stranglehold of the few, thus increasing the speed and quality of innovation and decision making, every day" (Linda A. Hill, 2014).

The Networked Business Structure. Some organizations are embracing this structure. It's vital to develop a structure to foster participation in the decision-making process The network structure is a new type of organizational structure viewed as less hierarchical (more "flat"), more decentralized, and more flexible than other structures. One of the advantages is it reduces over departmentation. The concept underlying the network structure is the social network; a social structure of interactions. Communication is more open and transparent. A disadvantage of the network structure is, it can lead to more complex relations in the organization.

6 | **Coaching:** Transformational leaders are keen on recognizing and developing the strengths of each follower. See the potential in others and provide them with the necessary training and coaching to lift them up. Transformational leaders assign and delegate work based on talents and interests, but also seek to move employees out of their comfort zones. The transformational leader uses coaching style to develop followers to attain higher levels of expertise and proficiency resulting in higher levels of performance. As a result, followers are brought to a place of higher levels of personal awareness. They see the transformational leader, as a mentor and coach and as someone who cares enough to push them to achieve their full. Such leaders want followers the opportunity to see meaning in their work and challenge them with high standards.

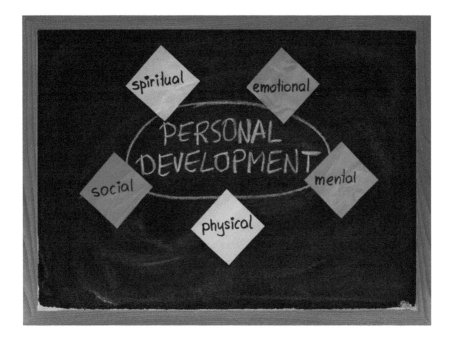

7 | **Personal Development.** Transformational leaders are committed to personal development to ensure that they are fulfilling their mission. You can't expect the organization to grow and improve unless you are willing to grow and develop. Such leaders value growth and always try to keep abreast of new changes in the marketplace and with their workforce. Additionally, they seek personal development (mental, spiritual, emotional, social and physical) to ensure they are performing at their optimum level. Growth must begin at the top.

8 | **Change.** Transformational times demand transformational leadership. Transformation, by definition, is about transitioning to something new. We live in times of great change, but that also means great opportunity. Companies need to be able to transform themselves much better and much faster. Look around, and you will see that disruption hits much harder and quicker than ever before. Today's most successful leaders understand

that the rate of change is rapid—and that it's not enough to plan for change. Studies show that leading companies in their corresponding sectors are those who have been most successful at implementing and capitalizing on major transformations when compared to competitors. Leaders must lead and inspire change. Transformational leaders foster innovation by challenging people to think outside the box. They promote taking calculated risks and learning from those mistakes. Our teams will only follow suit when they see their leaders embracing a culture of risk taking. A transformational approach to leadership unlocks the potential of your team.

The success of transformational leadership is wholly dependent on successful change leadership– the means by which leaders of the organization prepare, execute, experience, and institutionalize the transformation of the business with the employees and stakeholders of the organization. Transformational leadership is facilitative of change because it contributes to organizational improvement, effectiveness and institutional culture (Barnett, McCormick & Conners, 2001).

Factors that support successful business transformations include:

> Create a detailed change management plan which incorporates specific actions regarding people; communication plans, processes and technologies that will be transformed, action plans, roles and responsibilities of individuals, timelines and metrics for tracking progress and results.

> Create a shared vision – Sharing a vision is a central role of a leader. Leaders play a critical role when it comes to change.

They must show personal commitment, and communicate a convincing vision. Inspiring and empowering people to accept change and believe in the shared vision is essential. You must provide a clear picture of the future, and of the benefits, the change will bring. A vision gives people the big picture of what the future will be like. Transformational leaders have intuitive appeal, as the leader is on the 'front line' advocating change for others; followers are attracted to this traditional societal view on how a leader should be (Northouse, 2010).

➢ Conduct a Gap Analysis – This is an important tool to determine what you need to do to meet the change objectives. *Assess the cultural landscape.* Identify the core values, beliefs and behaviours that must be taken into account for the successful change to occur. Persuading people to change their behaviour won't avail for transformation unless formal elements—such as structure and ways of operating are redesigned to support them. Determine what steps need to be taken to move from the current state to the desired future state.

➢ Start at the top and involve very layer. Creating the business case; articulate the rationale for the business transformation, its objectives, its measurable value, and the benefits, risks, and costs to the organization. Enlist support from senior executives and management at lower tiers. It is critical for those individuals who have strong roles within the organization's power structure to sign up as vocal advocates for the business change.

➢ Identify rationales for objection that those resistant to the change may raise and construct responses to these before engaging the change effort. A comprehensive knowledge of the organization's culture and the people is needed for this. For example, let us suppose your team has been using email for managing their projects. And, now you recommend upgrading to a project management tool. Unless you can put forward the benefits of this new system, they will have an inclination to resist this change. But, once they know the change is going to make their life a lot easier, they will most likely support it.

➢ Create a schedule to provide regular and constant updates during the transformation. Leaders are expected to act as change agents and overcome resistance to the organizations initiatives. Communication should be simple and heartfelt; thereby, speaking to anxieties, confusion and distrust. Supply realistic details of both the positives and negatives of the change, and provide key information on a consistent basis. Maintain regular review meetings and adapt the organization's meeting structure and agendas to support the improved processes.

➢ Address the 'human side': Make the logical and emotional case together. People respond to calls to action that engage their hearts, as well as their minds. It makes them feel as if they are a part of something substantial. Most employees resist change due to job insecurity, mistrust of management, increased workload, and fewer opportunities for advancement. Leaders must show commitment to the change initiative, but above all, to the people who are affected by the change. This requires relationship building; thus, leaders must display authenticity, integrity, empathy, and humility in their approach.

➢ Training and Coaching: Use hands-on training to achieve understanding, involvement and commitment. Change, such as new structures, policies and acquisitions, creates new systems and environments. Assess training needs driven by the change. By comparing existing skills and competencies with the skills you want people to have, you can make an informed decision about the type of training each individual or team needs and provide the necessary training.

➤ Rewards and Recognition. If leaders are to promote and sustain positive behavioural change, a simultaneous change in the performance management process must be accompanied. Leaders should be clear about the underlying behaviours that will best support the new way of doing things, and find opportunities to perfect those behaviours. Rewards and incentives are reinforcers of behaviours. Without positive reinforcement in the midst of change, engagement and employee morale are at risk.

➤ Monitoring and Evaluation: Prepare for the unexpected. The stage is crystallizing the adaptation of a new standard as the norm. Change will only reach its full effect if it's made permanent, so every effort must be made to cement it. No change programme goes completely according to plan. It's essential to recognize that the change journey is not a straight line. Leaders need to make the adjustments necessary to maintain momentum and drive.

Teamwork

Bernard Bass identified that the key characteristic of this style of leadership is to motivate and inspire people and to direct positive change in groups. This style of leadership is linked to bringing groups together to work as teams, transformational leadership is seen as powerful when managing conflict and team performance (Zhang et al., 2011). Transformational Leadership engages employees by appealing to more intrinsic motivations such as a sense of purpose, fulfilment, autonomy and the nurturing of team spirit. Team members will unite to achieve the common goal, and this cohesiveness is what can motivate an individual to give up self-interest to advance the group's mission. Together, heightened effort and commitment lead to greater productivity. Transformational leadership is seen as effective as it gets groups to work to a common unified goal. Through doing this it also inspires followers to accomplish what is expected of them both individually and as a team (Northouse, 2013).

Lee Iacocca is a transformational leader who is credited with saving the Chrysler Corporation. He took over Chrysler when it was on the brink of bankruptcy and set about transforming the ideals of his closest subordinates. In turn, that began to reshape the corporation's culture. Because a transformational leader encourages others to become transformational leaders, soon the entire organization was filled with effective leaders (Kelly, 2003).

Another transformational leader is Lou Gerstner who will always be known as the man who saved IBM after reviving, then bolstering, the near bankrupt company when he took over as chairman and CEO in 1993. He turned IBM around from $8.1 billion loss in 1993 after identifying part of the company's problem as 'success syndrome'. That is, having been one of the greatest commercial institutions on Earth from the 1960s-1980s, IBM had become insular and rigid (Sheppard, 2002). Gerstner completely transformed the culture of the organization through, for example, modeling desired behaviour and abolishing IBM's notorious dress code to reflect better the attire of their customers (Sheppard, 2002).

"When I arrived at IBM, one of my first questions was, "Do we have teamwork?," because the new strategy crucially depended on our ability to provide an integrated approach to our customers. "Oh, yes, Lou, we have teamwork," I was told. "Look at those banners up there. Mr. Watson put them up in 1938; they're still there. Teamwork!" "Oh, good," I responded. "How do we pay people?"

"Oh, we pay on individual performance." The rewards system is a powerful driver of behavior and therefore culture. Teamwork is hard to cultivate in a world where employees are paid solely on their individual performance." —Lou Gerstner

Criticisms of Transformational Leadership

A key criticism is that transformational leadership has the potential for the abuse of power (Hall, Johnson, Wysocki & Kepner, 2002). Transformational leaders motivate followers by appealing to their emotions and may not necessarily attend to positive moral values. This power can be used to inspire individuals to follow an unethical or immoral leader (Northouse, 2010). Another criticism is that transformational leadership style lacks conceptual clarity as it covers such a wide range of key aspects that cannot be concreted (creating vision, building trust, motivation, changing agent) (Hall, Johnson, Wysocki & Kepner, 2002). However, when this style is used with an emphasis on the good, the results are tremendous; the leader, followers, organization and society will greatly benefit.

It must be said that transformational leadership must not be considered a substitute for a transactional approach. It 'augments' this style and enhances the leader's ability to work towards the attainment of organizational goals more effectively. Contingent rewards must be used with transformational leadership. Leaders need to balance both styles of leadership to achieve the best result.

The Future of Transformational Leadership

Sanders, Hopkins and Geroy (2003) propose an extension to both transactional and transformational leadership through what they call 'transcendental leadership'. Their model suggests three structural levels of leadership accomplishment, these being transactional: transformational, and transcendental. They propose that a leader's development is along three dimensions of spirituality – consciousness (mind), moral character (heart) and faith (soul). They contend for organizations and society to recognize the need for and embrace spirituality.

Conclusion

Transformational leadership is seen as a process that changes and transforms individuals (Northouse 2004). Leaders exert a remarkable level of influence that motivates followers to accomplish more than what is expected of them. This current technology driven era coupled with an unstable economic environment requires a more enlightened form of leadership to keep employees motivated. The primary focus of the transformational leadership style is to make change happen in ourselves, others, the organization and society. Leadership is about growth; improving oneself and going to a higher level. Transforming is a process. Everything happens in stages. Transformational leadership can improve an organizations performance as leaders place more emphasis on the people who give the organization its competitive advantage. It takes a long-term view to the with regards to employee development, motivation and retention. Burns (1979) states that a small well lead group of individuals can produce effective and efficient results even under high levels of stress. Transformational Leadership fosters a climate that encourages growth (personal and organizational). It enhances creativity and innovation which helps in the continuous improvement and transformation of the organization.

SECTION THREE

Leadership in Focus:
A Deeper Look at Yourself

CHAPTER TEN

ESCAPE THE LEADERSHIP DRIFT

A couple was on vacation, and they were floating in the ocean on inflatable rafts. The husband decided to head back to the shore, but his wife wanted to remain and catch some more rays of sunlight. After a while, the woman lost herself floating on the raft. What she failed to realize was that she was slowly drifting out to sea. As she completely relaxed, the gentle currents were taking her away with it. Her situation was becoming more and more unsafe. By the time she recognized how far out at sea she was, it was almost too late. The shore was further than she expected and she was terrified. Fortunately, in the end, the lifeguards were able to rescue her, but the whole situation could have been avoided if she wasn't careless.

Leadership Drift is an important area that we must reflect on if we are to come closer to the leaders we are meant to be. How many leaders are today, just coasting along in their leadership journeys? How many have drifted their way to a loss of vision? How many are not where they need to be? We have a culture that's drifting and many leaders routinely drift from their purpose, and many never return to their original mission. Drifting may lead you into the middle of the ocean, at a destination you did not intend. The problem is that the onset of drifting is subtle, and requires that you continuously focus. Leadership has drifted in our times to something that has a familiar face but deep down the true essence of leadership is being lost.

If you put a frog in a pot of hot water, it will immediately jump out. But if you put it in cold water and then turn on the heat, the water gradually warms up so that the frog goes to sleep not noticing that the water is getting hotter and hotter until the frog eventually dies.

Think back to your younger years when you started on your leadership journey:

> ➢ **Has there ever been a time in your life, when you were more excited about your leadership vision?**

> ➢ **Has there ever been a time that you were more committed to that vision than you are right now?**

> ➢ **Has there ever been a time when you felt a deeper sense of fulfilment about your daily work?**

If you answered yes to any of these three questions, you are in the process of drifting. Your light is dimming.

We do not arrive at our desired destination in life and business by accident. Without having our leadership deeply anchored in the right harbour, drifting happens to all. No leader is exempt from the danger of drifting away from their personal leadership philosophy. There are many currents in the leadership journey. Then there is time. Time changes us all. Many leaders unconsciously have slid away from their earlier better self. They keep appearances, but the years have carried them down the stream, turning them into someone no one will be able to recognize without their mask. Technology continues to upgrade but today's leader seems to be downgrading.

A loose connection. Paul Johnson told a leadership seminar class that while he was overseas, he received a car that gave trouble to start. For two months, he fussed over this car. When his replacement came, Johnson informed him about the car's temperament. Curious, his successor looked under the hood. "Dr. Johnson!" he exclaimed. "The only trouble with this car is a loose cable!" After tightening the line, Johnson's successor got into the car and turned the key. The vehicle blasted to life. The power had been there all the time. Only a loose connection prevented Johnson from using it. It is so easy to turn the searchlight on others instead of on our self. We are prone to blame others or something for our lack of power.

4 Reasons Leaders Drift

1 **Losing touch with the people** you are leading and the customers you are serving. Are you awake, present and engaged? Unfortunately, some leaders alienate themselves once they have achieved the position they have worked tirelessly to attain. They may rely on those second in command to maintain control and give direction. The problem is that leaders become dependent on those individuals who establish a mode of control where they are the ones who are pushing a self-centred agenda. It's important to pay attention, be observant and engage with your team and customers.

2 **Lack of Balance.** Ignoring the laws of health such as diet, nutrition, rest, and exercise, will sap your energy and weaken you physically and emotionally. Such leaders' lives are out of balance. They lose touch with those closest to them, their spouses, family and friends and eventually, they lose their ability to think logically about important issues. At your weakness moment, you then begin to drift slowly. Negative forces as failure, criticism, disappointments, rejection begin to beat you down and take the steam out of your engine. Additionally, the longer it is taking to achieve goals can wear you out. Sometimes we start out with clarity and then allow momentum to take over. Are you operating in automatic pilot mode or are you consciously navigating your ship?

A particular harbour in Italy can be reached only by sailing up a narrow channel between dangerous rocks and shoals. Over the years, many ships have been wrecked, as navigation is hazardous. Three lights were mounted on three huge poles in the harbour to guide the ships safely into port. When all the lights were perfectly lined up and seen as one, the ship could safely proceed up the narrow channel. If the pilot saw only two or three lights, he knew he was off course and in danger.

3 **Mixed up Priorities.** Whether it's being sucked into our career or focusing on wealth generation at the expense of other priorities, the question that should be asked is; "What is more important to me?" "Is it prestige and material possessions or the people I am leading?" Be clear about what matters most and where you want to go. When you take your focus off people and place them on things, you begin managing solely for results without connection to purpose. Here is where greed and selfishness can take over. Leaders can drift when they allow their power to corrupt their choices. Additionally, when we continuously seek approval from others, we begin to follow their path instead of our own. In our daily tasks, we can also drift when we allow ourselves to get distracted from doing the important things that will drive our success. We can get caught up doing tasks that were far from urgent or important, and in reality, are distracting us from what we should be doing.

4 **Remaining in your comfort zone.** You are no longer inspired by the overriding sense to fulfil the mission. You are comfortable with where you have reached, and the level of success and goals you have accomplished. You are not seeking risks anymore. Drifting can also be attributed to boredom. You are not being challenged. You have become sluggish and remain where you are. The many obstacles in your path have taken its toll on, weakening your resolve to press on.

You are burnt out; therefore, comfort and stability are embraced. You are neither cold nor hot. You have become lukewarm. The fizz has gone out of leading. When you remain in your comfort zone, you are in danger of unconsciously drifting from the anchorage of your leadership purpose. The tepid condition of the drifter is more dangerous than if he/she had been cold. Lukewarm leadership preserves enough of the form, and even of the content of the mission, however, renders leaders oblivious to the diligent effort necessary to the attainment of the high ideal of a successful journey. The typical lukewarm leader is content with things as they are and proud of the progress he/ she has made. It is almost impossible to convince them of their great need and of how far they are from their goal. Apathy is the nerve gas that paralyzes and prevents us from achieving goals. The truth is, we cannot lead with one foot on the shore and the other foot in the sea. You must get both feet wet. We cannot give a half-hearted effort. Leadership is not static. It's dynamic. You must be passionate about serving others.

"Progress means getting nearer to the place you want to be. And if you have taken a wrong turning, then to go forward does not get you any nearer. If you are on the wrong road, progress means doing an about-turn and walking back to the right road; and in that case the man who turns back soonest is the most progressive man."—C.S. Lewis

There's an expression in English: "to be painted into a corner." Imagine painting the floor of an apartment room but then realizing that you have ended up in a corner and cannot get out—except by stepping on the fresh paint. You have to stay there until it dries! Sometimes our actions seem to paint us into a corner. We arrive at a situation, and, like the wet paint on the floor, our actions or lack of it "traps" us.

Results of Drifting

1 Loss of Growth - We are meant to grow stronger and wiser in our leadership journey. We lose the potential to be all that we can be. Leadership is not a state of ease. Leaders cannot afford to be lethargic. "To whom much is given, much is required." There can be no life without growth. It's so hard to look at yourself objectively and accept that you haven't been growing or progressing.

2 Delay in Achieving goals – You don't get a prize if you started the race well but stopped in the middle, you must endure, to the end. When we live at a lower level, we miss out on the benefits of achieving our vision. It takes time, and a lot of work and energy to get back on track. Sadly due, to the extent of your drifting, you may have to start over again to build your reputation and gain trust.

3 Loss of values. You lose the core of yourself—who you really are and also being the best version of yourself. When leaders do not have clarity of thought about where they are going, their values and talents, they have a tendency to seek the quick fix as a solution to solve uncertainty. "If you find a path with no obstacles, it probably doesn't lead anywhere." —Frank A. Clark

4 | Missed Opportunities. You become distracted by issues that are not central to the role and responsibilities of being a leader. Key decisions may have been fumbled. When we drift we lose opportunities we otherwise would have taken. Our vision gets blurred, and our focus succumbs to short-term gains. This can lead to failure.

We send our organizations on an altered course. Lee Iacocca stated, *"The speed of the boss* is the speed of the team."* In a small town, the clock in the jeweller's window stopped one day at a half an hour to eight. Many of the residents had been depending on this clock to know the time. On one particular morning, many individuals glanced in the window and noticed it was only thirty minutes to eight; children on their way to school were surprised to find they still had plenty of time to stroll. Many individuals were late that morning because this central clock in the jeweller's window had stopped. As leaders we are to be the model "clock" of our organization. Everyone is looking to us since we set the pace. Employees are following your lead. When you drift, it affects everyone. Employees may be confused about the direction the organization is heading and how their actions fit into the big picture.

Years ago, Friedrich Nietzsche wrote about a madman who shouted in a marketplace, "What were we doing when we unchained this earth from the sun? Whither is it moving now? Whither are we moving? Away from all suns? Are we not plunging continually? Backward, side-ward, forward, in all directions? Is there still any up or down? Are we not straying, as through an infinite nothing? Do we not feel the breath of empty space?" His point was that all genuine foundations had been shattered, leaving us to wander aimlessly in all directions through a purposeless nothingness.

A leader doesn't drift into greater health or better focus. It takes no effort to cruise into the unknown, but it's hard to master having the drift bring you to your desired outcome. The currents that are in the ocean that many captains face - they need precise steering and high engine power to resist them.

Organizational Drift

Drift occurs on both a personal level and an organizational level. On an organizational level, drift is characterized by a slow deterioration of standards and operating principles and is often accompanied with rationalization. Organizations tend to drift from the mission, vision, rules, safe practices, procedures and lose focus. It can be the result of the pressures of competition and the desire to get to and stay at the top. Leaders tend to justify deviations. The organization becomes comfortable with a level of performance that is less than adequate or ethical - the end justifies the means. Drift requires detection and intervention. In retrospection and with the appropriate response, the vessel can be steered in the right direction.

For over a 100+ years following its founding in 1869, Goldman Sachs was viewed as the prudent model company on Wall Street. They zealously protected their client's interest and pursued long-term goals over short-term gains. According to Steven G. Mandis' fantastic book "What Happened to Goldman Sachs," the bank wasn't always viewed as unethical. In fact, in 1979, John Whitehead, then Co-Chair of Goldman, put forth 12 principles that guided the bank in its operations. Chief among these principles was the following statement: "Our client's interests always come first. Our experience shows that if we serve our clients well, our own success will follow." All of this changed in 1999 when the US Congress removed the barriers between investment and commercial banks. The leadership team at Goldman Sachs had to make a choice: either stay small and get crumpled by this new competition or play the game. They chose

223

the latter, and the transition from trusted advisor to unscrupulous traders began. The implication was that Goldman Sachs ethics relied on legal standards and not the "clients' interest first" principle that the firm historically observed. They drifted away from their original guiding principle because no one noticed that the company was drifting. Here we see what happens when a company shifts paradigms from its original one of focusing on customer needs/satisfaction to one of giving pre-eminence to shareholder value. This is the dilemma created by the simplistic financially dominated EVA (earned value analysis) and SVA (shareholder value analysis) model that factors out customer experience from the equation to emphasize revenues and cash flows. A simple two-dimensional matrix that incorporates non-financial variables could readily show more realistic optimum points than only monetary ones. The truth is no organization sets out to drift down a destructive path. The path is paved with good intentions. However, in a startlingly short amount of time, small compromises can transform the ethical foundation of an organization. It is easy to lose one's moral compass and become ungrounded. It is crucial that you surround yourself with people who are not afraid to call you out when they notice you aren't acting ethically. If you don't have this sound support system, it's very easy to lose your way and forget the repercussions of your decisions, and the reasons that you do what you do. Slowly, silently, and with little fanfare, organizations routinely drift from their purpose, and many never recover. Leaders must have the right principles and values when chosen for a leadership position. That will include their ways of dealing with aspects of the position which push or tempt them to compromise. Goldman was sharply criticized, in the aftermath of the 2007–2012 global financial crisis, where some believed that it misled its investors and profited from the collapse of the mortgage market. That time — "one of the darkest chapters" in Goldman's history (according to the New York Times—brought investigations from the Congress, the Justice Department, and a lawsuit from the U.S. Securities and Exchange Commission—to whom it agreed to pay $550 million to settle.

Overcoming the Leadership Drift

"Nothing is so easy as to deceive one's self; for what we wish, we readily believe." —Demosthenes. The easiest people to fool are ourselves. While it's not hard to be open, and candid about others faults, it's not so simple when we have are faced with our own. The human capacity for self-deception is startling. Maybe it's because we're so close to ourselves that it's difficult to see ourselves for who we truly are. Whatever the reason, facing especially our faults, is always painful.

A revival and a reformation must take place. Revival signifies a renewal of your leadership walk, an awakening of mind and heart and a resurrection from spiritual blindness. Reformation signifies a change in ideas, behaviours, and practices. Take concrete and practical steps to avoid the things that lead you to drift. The first step is to take stock. You will never be able to embrace change until you recognize your personal need. There will never be a greater movement in your life if you are satisfied with where you are right now. Reclaiming your purpose is important. We must also remember our early stages when our fire was burning brightly. Let that feeling ignite you and awaken that desire to lead passionately. Passion is indeed oxygen to the soul. Return to the practices that helped you to grow and develop as a leader. The law of thermodynamics tells us that the physical world is decaying and that the direction of all creation is downward. If we do not apply a pro-active counter-effort in life and business, the natural course of events will lead us to drift downstream like a raft in a river. Additionally, as the river flows downward, it widens. There is no telling where you could end up.

To get out of drifting demands that you continuously focus and "fight the current" to avoid floating downstream. It requires you to take time out for yourself to pause, reflect and re-calibrate (mentally and spiritually). You need clarity about your purpose, your priorities, your values, and vision. Nothing is more important to leadership than a degree of self-awareness, an ability to reflect and analyze whether you are on top of your game. Lastly, we need to turn away from our neglect of our personal leadership philosophy and make that commitment to be mindful and remain focused. Conscious leadership is not accidental. It is intentional. Going upstream takes work. You never drift against the tide.

Leaders must establish standards. Every time my family visit the beach we position our slippers on the shore, then head into the ocean. Only when we look up at our spot on the beach, could we tell we had moved. We didn't notice or even feel we were drifting. Leadership drift happens all the time and without awareness. It's good to have a landmark (constant) to evaluate your position. Accountability keeps us in check. We don't drift off course overnight. Drift often happens in small and subtle ways. Left unchecked, it eventually becomes significant. We may start out not realizing anything is amiss or wrong. One little thing occurs, and we justify it. Something else happens again. Subtly boundaries and good judgment may get lost for a while until or unless there is some awakening, either from within or coming from the outside. We need to be consistently reflecting and evaluating where we are drifting, and if we realize we are, we need to find a way to get back on track before it's too late.

A few years ago a freighter sailing from Great Britain to the coast of France was experiencing engine problems. Just off the French coast, the engines had completely failed, and the ship was beginning to drift at sea. The problem was that the tides were pulling the ship to the shore and a rocky shoreline that would inescapably cause the ship to crash. Such an accident could cause the loss of cargo, the loss of the entire ship or even the loss of life. The reason for this situation was neglect of proper care of the engines. Sadly, those in charge forgot to check the oil and let it run out. The reason the engines shut down was due to a lack of lubricant.

How is your engine going? Is it firing on just one, or operating on all cylinders? Let's put some work into our personal leadership philosophy, the driving force in our leadership journey so that we can be all that we are meant to be and who our followers need us to be. Drifting through life is a real danger. We need to be more deliberate with our time, talents and resources. If you develop self-awareness, build your support system with genuine people and adhere to moral and ethical principles you can stay on track and avoid the leadership drift pitfall.

CHAPTER ELEVEN

LEADERSHIP FRAMEWORK:
A HOUSE BUILT TO LAST

FAITH

WISDOM

HUMILITY

AUTHNETICITY

INTEGRITY

HOPE

GOALS & STRATEGY

VISION & MISSION

LOVE

Building your leadership dream house can be one of the most challenging and rewarding endeavours you can undertake. It is prudent to follow a building plan, although you can never be fully prepared or estimate the full cost due to the uncertainty of the journey. Taking the scope of the venture into account before you get started can help make the process go more efficiently.

THE FOUNDATION

LOVE - Leadership that is built on shifting sand as an emotional high, or other unstable surfaces as greed and selfishness will likely fail over a period. Your foundation must be based foremost on love; a genuine care and concern for people. Being a Leader is a matter of getting our priorities right. It's putting people before technology. People are the greatest asset to any organization. They are the ones who must implement, commit and transform the organization. Put people first, and everything else will fall into place. Our motives and purpose for leading must be pure. To look after others solely for their own good, with no selfish motives, is to reveal true leadership. Love has the power to transform us. Love is the supreme virtue of leaders. It is love that motivates us to give ourselves selflessly so others can enjoy the fruits of our labour. Love must be central to our character. Love may be one of the most misunderstood and misused words in our language, and it is used so lightly today. We often say that we love to hike, we love to eat, we love movies and in the same breath, we say we love our children. We love things and use people when it should be the other way around. But genuine love is something altogether different, something that impacts our entire existence, our way of life, our way of relating to others. It is love in action, involving the mind and heart.

Love cannot occur without action, and every act strengthens and extends it. To love someone as ourselves means to take care of someone else the same way you would take care of yourself. Unless we daily cultivate the precious fruit of love we are in danger of becoming unsympathetic, selfish and proud. True love is always active. It is a way to serve others while at the same time edifying and uniting your team. The law of love is the foundation of leadership. We do not coerce others to follow us. We want them to do so of their free will. Mother Theresa beautifully illustrated this concept of leadership when she was invited to speak at a leadership conference. "If you want to lead your people, you first have to understand them. If you want to understand your people, you have to love them. Do you love your people? Ultimately, it is not the magnitude of our actions that matters but the amount of love that we put into them." Love is power. The value of pure love resides in its focus to do good and to do nothing else than good. When one looks around the world, the fruits of hate is destructive. Love is like a fire that warms the soul, a light that shines, a fragrance that revives and a magnet that draws people. Love should prompt everything the leader does. Love embraces every duty to serve others. Love is like an artesian well. We do not need a container or a pump to bring the water up. It flows freely. It cannot be clogged. True love seeks to help, never to hurt. However, the love we display to any one particular individual should not blind or cover up that person's faults. Love must at times come in the form of discipline. One of the best ways in which love can show itself is by giving counsel. Genuine counsel benefits the receiver even if it is unfavourable.

British writer William Somerset Maugham once said that "the greatest tragedy of life is not that men perish, but that they cease to love." We live in a time which less emphasis is placed on endeavouring to live the life of self-less service to others. It's all about what is in this for me. It's incredible how much people strive to succeed in a career or make money, yet they don't strive to leave a positive legacy although death is the only assurance in life. The pull toward self-centeredness is strong. We never seem to acquire quite enough. We tell ourselves sometime in the near future we'll contribute our time, talents, and money. The word love is used so often that it is easy to lose sight of what it truly means. Love is something we do rather than just an emotion. Love motivates us to action. In spite of it all, love never fails. Think for a moment of what our organizations would be like if we consistently practiced the qualities of love for one another. Imagine the beauty of working in an environment where the team members are genuinely positive and affirming of each other. Love is the most powerful force in all of creation. We are not meant to enjoy this blessing of leadership by ourselves. We are to pass it along to and enjoy it with others. Throughout all ages, the true strength of leadership has been in the love that leaders have for their followers and the future generations.

Love is being of service to others. Albert Schweitzer (1875-1965), a physician and philanthropist who served in Gabon, Africa, once told a group of students: "I do not know which will be the destiny of each one of you; but one thing I know—the only ones among you who will be really happy will be those who have sought and found the way to serve."

There are so many business books and articles giving advice how to be a great leader, but few ever mention love. It sounds kind of soft and doesn't go well with the assertiveness we see that is needed to take you to the top in today's world. Yet if we have love at the heart of leadership we would be better leaders and have better relationships with the people we lead and with our customers. Not only is love the best business plan underlying any strategy, but it's also the most motivating concept that will lift your team and take them to meaningful heights. Love can change the world.

We feel it in our hearts, and see it in our homes, but why don't really see it at work?

Somehow this powerful force of love has been placed on the back burner and downgraded to second-class status. In Hebrew, the word for love is *ahava*, which is three letters combined, meaning "I give". When you put love into practice, you know your place in the universe. Love doesn't shy away from challenges. It's courageous and considers work and service the same thing. When you love, you give it all; you leave it wherever you are. Love is the one word that can differentiate you in leadership as someone who truly cares to make a positive impact in the lives of others. Love cannot exist without expression. By putting it front and centre of your leadership, you can become a source of hope, inspiring people in ways they never thought possible. Don't let today's norm of being egotistical hinder you from applying the power of love. Love is the adhesive that binds all other virtues into a united whole and gives authenticity to all we do. Leaders who stand on the foundation of love, don't only take into consideration the balance sheets when making decisions but also the humane side and this is what is prominently missing in our corporate self-seeking world today. It's about connecting goals with how they'll positively impact the lives of others.

We are in the age of information, and although we have gained so much knowledge, selfish motives can sometimes get the best of us, and so much of that knowledge and new power gained has been a source of suffering. We are so busy trying to create meaning in our own life that we forget the journey is about helping others. Power and knowledge in and of themselves aren't necessarily bad. It's what people do with them. The leader of a powerful country has a lot of power. He can use that power to build houses or make weapons of mass destruction. Some of us have enemies or are regarded by others as their enemies. It is important to analyze our relationships and do some introspection to ascertain why those relationships have broken down and what can be done to repair them. As leaders, we are challenged to build positive relationships, even with those we do not like. Mahatma Gandhi (1869-1948) once stated, "It is easy enough to be friendly to one's friends. But to befriend the one who regards himself as your enemy is the quintessence of true religion."— Non-Violence in Peace and War (New York: New Directions Pub. Corp., 1965)

During the First World War, the Society of Friends printed "Jesus Christ, The Sermon on the Mount" as a pamphlet for distribution among the allied forces. But both the British and French governments prohibited its distribution among their troops. After all, a sermon telling soldiers to love their enemies was not exactly what they had wanted men on the battlefields of war to be reading. Our world is filled with hurt and very sensitive people. After all, who has not—however inadvertently—offended or hurt someone and at times those whom they love the most? Even so, who has not been hurt by those whom they love the most? It is one of the common facts of life that it is easy to offend; it is even easier to be offended. What's not so easy is to forgive. If only forgiveness came as easy as the offence. The message of love has relevance for our relationship with those whom we dislike or, even worse, might even feel hatred towards. Loving our enemies does not come naturally. Someone once said: "Loving our enemies, then, does not mean that we are supposed to love the dirt in which the pearl is buried; rather it means that we love the pearl which lies in the dust." Forgiveness is a strategic issue. All too often, forgiveness becomes optional, something we extend or withhold or refuse to accept because we would prefer to remain resentful. Some time ago, Lewis Smedes wrote an article titled "Forgiveness: The Power to

Change the Past." In it, Smedes writes, "When you forgive someone, you slice away the wrong from the person who did it. You disengage that person from his hurtful act. You recreate him. At one moment you identify him ineradicably as the person who did you wrong. The next moment you change that identity. He is remade in your memory."

There's a story told about the great English Admiral Lord Nelson, who, right before a significant naval battle, took two disputing officers to a location where they could see all the enemy ships gathered to make war against them. "Yonder," said the admiral, "are your enemies. Shake hands and be friends like good Englishmen." In other words, the concerns at stake were too high to let personal differences stand in the way of triumph.

Imagine what our organizations would be like were we to, indeed, reflect these principles! Imagine what it would be like if we would learn to think of others before ourselves; imagine if we showed others, unconditional love, even when they didn't deserve it. Imagine if we forgave those who hurt us. Imagine if we were as attentive to the welfare of others as we were about our own affairs. Although implementing these principles would not solve all our leadership problems, we face today, no doubt they would greatly help!

> "Take the first step in faith. You don't have to see the whole staircase, just take the first step." —Martin Luther King Jr.

STAIRS

These are the steps that allow you to move forward. This elevation will prevent the floods of doubt and fear from cancelling your dream in this initial stage.

> **Vision & Mission**. Vision is future oriented. Having a clear vision of where you are going is crucial in any human endeavour. A mission is the statement of purpose. It's the reason for your existence. It is designed to guide the everyday actions of and decisions made by a leader.

> **Goals and Strategy**. A goal is a specific aim that the leader works toward. Goals have certain results that are achievable and measurable. They can either be short term or long term. Once you have drafted the goals, you can formulate a strategy for getting there. Strategy is your blueprint or plan of action designed to achieve the goals. You can't inspire others to follow you if the direction is not clear.

THE FOUR PILLARS

You must build uphold your leadership structure on these 4 qualities (hope, humility, integrity and authenticity). These posts build your teams' trust and confidence in you which is needed to influence them. If you ignore any one of these pillars, your leadership effort will eventually crumble.

➢ **Humility** allows one to set their ego aside. Humility is the ceasing to fight for your own agenda, but rather that of the multitude. The humble leader is not occupied with self. Many leaders mistake controlling, dominating, or other harsh behaviours for strength. Humility takes strength and is the opposite of pride and arrogance; it is the mastery of self-leadership. When consistently pursued and prudently polished over time, it is a powerful force for good that helps to sustain success. Humble leaders are great listeners and welcome feedback. Scientific research into the power and effectiveness of humility has shown that it offers a significant "competitive advantage" to leaders.

When asked by one of his disciples about the ingredients of good government, Confucius answered:" 'Sufficient food, sufficient weapons, and the confidence of the common people.'

"'But,' asked the disciple, 'suppose you had no choice but to dispense with one of those three, which would you forego?'

"'Weapons,' said Confucius.

"His disciple persisted: 'Suppose you were then forced to dispense with one of the two that are left, which would you forego?'

"Replied Confucius, 'Food. For from of old, hunger has been the lot of all men, but a people that no longer trusts its rulers is lost indeed.'"—Edited by Michael P. Green, 1500 Illustrations for Biblical Reading (Grand Rapids, Mich.: Baker Books, 1989)

➤ **Authenticity** means being genuine and not putting on a show. Trust includes the willingness to commit oneself to the care of the one trusted. A dictionary defines trust as complete assurance regarding the character, ability, strength, or truth of someone or something. Trust involves placing confidence in someone, believing in that person and relying totally on her or his integrity. Leadership is the ability to influence others which is based upon trust. If you want your team to trust you and you want their commitment, you will need to be authentic. Living authentically is a noble path that you won't regret following. Authentic leadership is a constant journey and commitment, both to your own growth and to the growth of others. Do you know how people really regard you? Effective leaders have a comfortable level of honest communication with their teams and a true understanding of how they are perceived. Testing others' perception of you can be done by observing their behaviour. Are your team members relaxed around you? Does all conversation stop when you enter the room?

"Ability may get you to the top, but it takes character to keep you there." — John Wooden

➤ **Integrity**. Research on leadership has consistently rated integrity as one of the most important character traits of a respected leader. Integrity, defined. "Adherence to moral and ethical principles, soundness of moral character. Integrity— is like a code of honour. If you are a person of integrity, you have certain values and beliefs that you live by. Integrity is one of the essential building blocks of character. It's keeping your word, being fair, giving credit where it's due, communicating honestly and being there when people need you. The story is told of a Greek philosopher named Diogenes of Sinope who walked the streets of Athens with a lantern; his ultimate goal being to find an honest man. According to one version of the story, he finally found someone whom he believed fit the description. Diogenes, however, was mistaken. The gentleman stole his lantern, and poor Diogenes had to find his way home in the dark.

"It's not what we eat but what we digest that makes us strong; not what we gain but what we save that makes us rich; not what we read but what we remember that makes us learned; and not what we profess but what we practice that gives us integrity." —Francis Bacon, Sr

> **Hope** is the cornerstone of leadership. Challenging times like these that we are facing are the most difficult in which to lead, especially as the workplace changes, the economy struggles, and employees live in fear and uncertainty of their jobs. People are challenged to remain motivated. The ability to instil hope is a necessary leadership trait. Giving hope to your people combines the alignment, engagement, and vision of the organization. Leadership is about having a vision for the future and hope enables people to look forward with anticipation and expectation towards that future state. Hope renews faith, promotes clarity and helps to improve productivity.

WALLS AND ROOF

> **Frame up walls with Commitment**. Commitment is the cement that holds the structure together. Feelings change, people will come and go and at times you may find yourself with few supporters but you will have to persevere to attain the vision. It all boils down to how much you really want it. You must be determined and demonstrate a strong work ethic.

> **Ceiling rafters of Wisdom**. This ties the roof and the pillars together. "All men by nature," wrote Aristotle, "desire to know." Learning is intended to make us wise. What, though, is wisdom? Wisdom is discernment, understanding and foresight. The ability to know when to switch between autocratic and democratic style with your team. Wisdom is the ability to use knowledge in a practical way. Wisdom means embracing continuous learning. It is also exercising self-control. Firstly, before one can lead an organization one

has to be able to govern his or her own self. True temperance is control over every phase of our life. Self-control is to character as mortar is to a brick building. The word temperance is an old English word used to indicate moderation. The Greek word for "temperate" comes from a word often used in the context of athletic training, of an athlete who, is preparing for an event and avoids that which can weaken their body and negatively affect their performance. Self-control refers to the strength of operating in the face of desires, temptations and wants. It is the ability to control one's emotions and behaviour in the face of external demands. How much more then should this principle apply to us leaders in our walk? As human beings, we are bestowed with a gift not found among other creatures, and that is reason. Yet, we are also creatures of emotion. Ideally, our reason should be used to guide our emotions and feelings however, such is not always the case. It is important that we keep a tight control over what goes on inside us because what's inside will ultimately be manifested on the outside. How often do we allow emotions or passions to cloud and override our judgment? This can have dire consequences. Feelings are fickle. The mind is the rudder for the body that we control. Take away the control of the mind, and we will be dominated by whatever feelings blow our way.

The British poet Alexander Pope once wrote about how "Pleasures are ever in our hands or eyes," and yet, when we do them, they cease to bring us the enjoyment we imagine. It's only in anticipation of doing them that they seem so enticing; in reality, they don't give us what we ultimately expected they would. It doesn't last so we need more and more of it to reach the same level of immediate satisfaction. Then we finally realize that there's much more to life than just pleasure and that pleasure alone leaves us empty and dissatisfied. A person without self-control has two difficulties: from outside as well as from inside. Such a person is like a country without borders that yields to outside enticements and attacks from every side. On the inside, he or she is like a fallen city that has no inward strength to resist. The leader's life is a battle and a march. The victory is gained by attainment of the vision and through self-leadership. But to control one's self, does not totally mean living a life of denial. We should not approach self-control from a negative perspective, but a positive one. If we don't control ourselves—our feelings—then they will control us. Synonyms for self-control include self-discipline, strength of mind, and willpower. It extends far beyond simply restraining from doing what's insincere but enables us to do what's good. The effects are long-lasting and produce a great reward. It may seem contradictory, but self-denial enhances personal freedom and, therefore, inner peace. Some leaders, in order to gratify ambition and desires, wound their conscience. Thus, their character is stained, and their life is an unending road of never having enough. The issue of discipline is a two sided coin. From time to time, we will have to discipline employees. We must do this with consistency, tact and compassion. We must also be receptive of discipline and learn how to accept correction in a mature and constructive manner. On the other hand, how do you react when accusations are levelled against you in your leadership position? Anger can make us irrational. When we lose our temper, we are not in control anymore. We are reacting rather than responding. Having temporarily thrown out the life principles we had so carefully cultivated, we say and do things we later regret. We look rather foolish. A bad temper can become a habit. As long as individuals operate on the basis of "one bad turn deserves another," they will continue the fight. This is the standpoint which destroys relationships "A soft answer turneth away wrath:

but grievous words stir up anger" (Proverbs. 15:1). If only someone would be big enough to let go of hurts and forgive. Lack of self-control in our society is constantly is promoted. Advertising tells us to gratify ourselves: "Why wait, why deny yourself, why sacrifice? Constantly we hear, "Indulge yourself because you deserve it." Self-control doesn't come in a day. It comes in hits and misses, in failures and successes, as we try to practice it daily. Moreover, don't put yourself in situations where your weaknesses will be tested, where you can easily succumb to temptation. We must avoid even the appearance of unethical behaviour. Self-awareness is vital to self-control. A businessman confessed to his pastor one day that he had become entangled in an illicit love affair. "I couldn't help it," he stated. "You wouldn't understand the outside pressures that were affecting me." The pastor responded: "You couldn't help it? Outside pressures? Whatever happened to your inside braces?"

➤ **The Roof of Faith**. While hope looks to the future, faith believes in the present. Let faith be your covering. One of the best descriptions of faith is found in Hebrews 11:1 — "Now faith is the substance of things hoped for, the evidence of things not seen." In our darkest hour, leaders need to be able to see what is obscure to our unaided sight. No matter how dark the night, we can be equipped to see the light. Behind every dark cloud, so the saying goes, is a silver lining. Genuine faith reaches beyond what we can see, feel and touch. As with the foundation, the roof is fundamental to the veracity of your leadership structure. Faith provides assurances in the present. Instability is the principal challenge as far as leadership goes, and our climate has become increasingly volatile. High winds of disappointment, heavy rainfall of failure, hail storms triggered by critics, and dense snowfall of rejection, can take their toll on your mind. Faith allows you to stand up to the rigours of your regional weather; to keep believing when everything tells you to give up. If your roof is leaking —that is a problem. Any amount of moisture (doubt, fears and discouragement) can result in damage to the roof's rafters and structural support, as well as to possessions in the interior. "In a discussion concerning the question of faith and reason, author John Hedley Brooke wrote about the German philosopher Immanuel Kant (1724–1804) and his attempt to understand the limits of human knowledge, notably when it came to the working of God. For Kant, "the question of justifying the ways of God to man was one of faith, not of knowledge. We can only do so much as humans. We are here today and gone in the twinkling of an eye. It is my faith in God that gives me hope and strength even when things don't go my way. Everyone has experienced the cravings associated with physical hunger and thirst. These needs can be easily satisfied with food or water but the hungering and thirsting of the soul leaves an inner emptiness. We cannot feed our spiritual life with physical food. Prayer is the source of spiritual power that connects us to God. A healthy prayer life is as necessary to sustain personal growth as breathing is to maintain our existence. I would say the secret to my success has been hard work and prayer. In my previous corporate position, I always exceeded expectations in my yearly performance appraisals. Every morning I would always say a prayer for my team, our customers and for the overall success of the company. As I look back on difficult situations with customers and the business which looked totally hopeless that had a positive outcome, I can only say it had to be the hand of God.

Many people always tell me I have a strong spirit and I am not easily ruffled. I trust God, and I put Him first in everything I do. This gives me great assurance and inner peace. When William IV of England died, Alexandrina Victoria was sleeping in the palace. After waking up to the news that she was now the Queen of England, she fell to her knees and prayed that the Lord would guide her through the years ahead. She became Queen in 1837 when she was just 18. Thus Queen Victoria became one of the greatest leaders in British history. Her reign lasted for more than 60 years.

"Faith is like radar that sees through the fog" —Corrie Ten Boom

DESIGNING THE INTERIOR

- ➢ **Rooms: Mental, Spiritual, Emotional, Physical**. "There is an Indian proverb or axiom that says that everyone is a house with four rooms, a physical, a mental, an emotional and a spiritual. Most of us tend to live in one room most of the time but, unless we go into every room every day, even if only to keep it aired, we are not a complete person." —Rumer Godden. One additional room that should be constructed is **Social**.

- ➢ **Windows of Communication**. Leaders must possess outstanding communication skills. Communication must be open, transparent and regular. It is a two-way street which includes feedback.

- ➢ **Doors of Creativity**. Step out of your comfort zone. Leadership is dynamic, not static. Charting new paths requires a healthy dose of risk- taking. Risks lead to opportunity. Great leaders take the right risks at the right time.

INSTALLING THE ESSENTIALS

> **Electricity and Lighting - Passion**. The word passion is defined as any powerful or compelling emotion or feeling. Passion is the driving force that propels us to action. It is the fire that burns within us and lights the way. It will energize you and induce others to follow and support your vision. As Ralph Waldo Emerson said, "Enthusiasm is one of the most powerful engines of success...Nothing great was ever achieved without enthusiasm."

> **Plumbing and water management—Controls in place**. Management focuses on the set of processes that keep an organization functioning. The great need for vision and inspiration (leadership) is a must, but equally, systems must be monitored and controlled to ensure that tasks and roadmaps are created to operationalize the vision. Without efficient management skills, the direction set by a leader risks being unsustainable.

> **Air-conditioning & Heating System—Competence**. Leaders are relied upon for their intelligence and expertise, which determines the quality of the performance of the organization. They must show competence. To perform effectively, leaders need to be knowledgeable about their fields and keep to abreast of the ever changing environment to be able to make more informed decisions. Above all, you are expected to deliver results.

FENCES

Your leadership framework must be enclosed in Teamwork. All great leaders are teachers. It's about training and coaching and making more leaders. It's about bringing people together and uniting them to work together for the common goal. Putting together strong teams that work well is a trait of great leaders. Your leadership vision is only sustainable via team effort.

Could this be your story? Tony and Betty saw a need. And they set about to fill it. Their creative passion brought fresh life to the community as they started a small non-profit organization. This venture brought them much fulfilment until a fateful meeting when Tony and Betty felt that most of the people did not appreciate their efforts. Five years had passed, but the string of constant criticism became too much for them. What happened next may sound familiar. They became disheartened and resigned from the outreach they had begun. No one stepped up to the plate, and within a few months, the doors to this establishment were closed.

A house is built upon a foundation, and its design and structure follow a set of plans. It has doors, windows, rooms, and a roof. Without these, it would not be a house. Leadership is costly (personally, physically, emotionally, and financially). Like anything else, we need to perform regular check-ups and maintenance to ensure all parts remain strong since 'wear and tear' happens. Without a strong foundation, roof and structure cracks will begin to surface, and your leadership efforts may fall apart. We live in a world today that is full of greed, hatred and selfishness, and an overall lack of social responsibility. We cannot fix the problems that exist in our society with the same thinking that created these problems. If we are to create a world of love, peace, patience, kindness, and self-control, we need first to change what we predominantly focus on and then transform ourselves. It is important to put our people before profits. Otherwise, we will continue on a more destructive path. We can make the difference by promoting what really matters - values that lead to happy, healthy, compassionate, and socially responsible individuals, communities, societies and organizations which will positively impact the world we live in. Follow this building plan to build a leadership structure that will stand the test of time. Eventually what started off as a house will become a home - by way of your legacy living on in the hearts and minds of followers.

CHAPTER TWELVE

PURPOSE DRIVEN LEADERSHIP: LEADING WITH THE HEART

The greatest tragedy in life is not death but a life without purpose.—Dr Myles Munroe

Everybody is driven by something; every leader is driven by something. As leaders, we seek for meaning, for a purpose, for direction, and sometimes in some strange ways, too. Here we are, in this world, with so many options, and so many paths to choose from. To have purpose is to give meaning to the goals we are striving to achieve. Your leadership purpose is the essence of who you are. The difference between average and successful leaders is their purpose. Your purpose and focus becomes your driver. Purpose is increasingly being called the key to navigating this multifaceted, unpredictable and uncertain world we live in today. The best leaders create an environment that allows people to succeed. They do this by having a deep awareness of their purpose. Purpose must tap into people's hearts and help them give their best when the odds are against them. You cannot achieve the goals that you have until you can establish your "WHY" factor. *It's your reason for doing what you are doing. "Why do I want to lead?" "What's the purpose of my leadership?"* Research States that fewer than 20% of leaders have a strong sense of their individual purpose.

The "5 Whys" technique can be very helpful in getting to the root of what you truly desire.

Make a chain of "Why?" questions. You ask yourself why you want to achieve a particular goal. For example, "Why do I want this position?" You might answer, "Because I want to advance in my career." Then ask again. "Why do I want to advance in my career?" Continue with "Why?" on each answer at least five times. Eventually, you will end up with your real motives and the deeper value behind your wishes. We can never know for sure the motives of others, but we can only work on ourselves and model the right way for others, leading by example.

One cold winter in South Wales, a mother was travelling cross-country with her baby and was caught in a terrible snowstorm. The next day, upon learning she never reached her destination, a search group went looking for her. They soon spotted a large bank of snow on the road. They quickly swept it away only to find the frozen body of the barely clothed woman. In her arms was her baby—alive and wrapped in a bundle of clothing. In the brunt of the snowstorm, the mother had removed most of her clothing and wrapped it around her baby to keep him alive. She knew that she would die, but that there was a chance the baby might survive. This baby boy grew up to become David Lloyd George, the revered Prime Minister of Britain during World War I. One of the reasons he achieved such great success is that he never forgot about his mother's sacrifice.

> ➤ **Take Time to Reflect**

❖ What are the things I believe in?

❖ What do I truly desire?

❖ What drives me?

"I had travelled eight thousand miles around the American continent and I was back on Times Square . . . with its millions and millions hustling forever for a buck among themselves, the mad dream—grabbing, taking, giving, sighing, dying, just so they could be buried in those awful cemetery cities beyond Long Island City."—Jack Kerouac, On the Road (New York: New American Library, 1957). Life, however, does not have to be so futile. We can make our leadership journey meaningful.

Begin to think about and consider what you want to see in the world (at work and in your personal life) that will make a positive difference. "Purpose is the most powerful motivator in the world. The secret of passion truly is purpose." —Robin Sharma

My leadership purpose is _____." It's about settings goals, long and short term. It's your personal mission statement. A purpose rises from your entity and is informed by the society's needs. Reflection is paramount. It can help you reconnect with your dreams. Set aside time daily to pause and reflect. You must be willing to look within yourself through regular self-reflection to strive for greater self-awareness. It's impossible to see the big picture and where you are if you keep going nonstop. The practice of visualizing can be very useful. One exercise I do every morning is to visualize that the goals I am working towards are happening. You must also visualize the impact you'll have on others as a result of living your purpose.

My leadership purpose ultimately comes from a desire to help others. This desire was formed quite early in my childhood. I was raised by my mother, a single parent together with my five other siblings. Things were incredibly difficult, and when my mother could no longer make ends meet, she sought help from the church. Thank God for their assistance. They provided food, clothing and even paid for my after school lessons. I often say I am a product of people giving back. I could not be where I am today without the help and support of others. Therefore, I use my leadership influence to inspire my team as well as bring awareness and support to the charitable needs of the community. As the words of one of my favourite hymn goes: "If I can help somebody as I pass along; then my living shall not be in vain."

> **Find Your Passion**

❖ What am I passionate about?

❖ What do I excel at?

❖ What do I want to do?

The next step is to identify your values, and passions and strengths; those pursuits that invigorate you and bring you joy. All to be guided towards a greater purpose. Your leadership purpose is who you are and what you're here to accomplish. There is some area of life you are meant to make a positive impact and complete that assignment. When you find your purpose, it will be easy to pursue it even in the face of obstacles because it is naturally embedded within you. It will flow smoothly like oil. It is something that even if you don't receive any money for, you will still continue doing. It will bring you great fulfilment. Your gifts are not to be used for selfish gain, but it's to edify others. Passion is contagious. Purpose-driven leaders ignite others to commit to the vision and to believe in the cause. **"The goal of 'The Purpose Driven Life' is to help people develop a heart for the world." —Rick Warren.**

> ➢ **Set Your Vision and Goals**

❖ Where do I see myself and the organization for the next 10 years, 5 years, 1 year and 6 months?

❖ What are the ways to make it happen?

❖ How is my life going to be in next 5 years if I fail to achieve those milestones?

The key to accelerating growth and strengthening your impact, in both your professional and personal lives is purpose. The process of finding out your purpose and finding the courage to live it, is the single most important progressive task you can embark on as a leader. Take the steps necessary to make your dreams happen. Set long term and short term goals. A team depends on its leader to tell them where they are going, why they are taking that particular course, and how they're going to reach the destination. People are more motivated when a leader articulates his or her vision for the organization, along with the steps and goals needed to achieve it.

➢ **Revisit your Character**

❖ What kind of person will I have to be to achieve the vision?

❖ Why are my actions important to the people I serve?

❖ How do I want to feel about myself?

Authenticity. Research suggests that 8 out of 10 people don't trust leaders. The challenges we face today are for the most part rooted in failures of leadership. Purpose-driven leaders embrace value-based leadership. They are authentic. They don't have one set of guidelines for when people are watching them, and another for when they're alone. Value-based leadership focuses on aligning an organization's values, mission and vision with its strategy, processes and systems. It is essentially about creating a culture of trust. Value-based leadership takes into consideration the whole organization, and it acts around well-defined core values. You must have the ability to identify and reflect on what you stand for, what your values are, and what matters most to you, then it becomes much easier to know what to do in any given situation. It always comes down to doing the right thing. How sincere are you in your leadership walk? A businessman was once heard to say, "I can't wait to get home at night, I get so tired of being nice to these common folks!" What a sad attitude to have towards the people we lead. The word hypocrite in the original language (hupokrites) means actor. We should be sincere in our leadership walk. The word sincere comes from two Latin words—sine (without) and cera (wax). Apparently, in the past, some sculptors would underhandedly fix the flaws and cracks in their work by plugging them with wax, which, doesn't hold for long. Therefore, sincerity means being real and genuine, not artificial. It means speaking "from the heart" and meaning it. Authenticity is important because the one who isn't sincere is someone with a divided heart. There is surely something else pulling on the leader and as such the motives cannot be in the right place.

Integrity & Honesty. Aristotle said that effective leaders must possess three things: ethos (character), logos (logic) and pathos (emotion). Ethos was foundational to the two other qualities as it served as the credibility factor of the leader. The Ethos Factor: Today this is what we call integrity. Honesty is truthfulness. It means you are not going to lie, cheat or steal. Honesty is a fundamental building block of a strong character and should be in play every day of our lives.

Our business deals must be above accusation, whether we privately sell a car or professionally engage in a business transaction. Indeed, whatever business we are in and whatever level at which we work, we should be honest, honourable, and fair. We must show honesty and integrity in all our financial dealings and with those whom we associate with. True leaders are concerned with the iceberg effect, the inner self which no one can see—Self-mastery. One of the greatest victories the leader can attain is the victory over self. And it is not until self is overcome that we can truly achieve altruism. Selfishness will negatively impact our relationships with others.

"I believe the most important attribute for a leader is being principle-centred. Cantering on principles that are universal and timeless provides a foundation and compass to guide every decision and every act." –Stephen R. Covey. There can be no difference between what you say and what you do. "Leaders who have a clearly articulated purpose and are driven to make a difference can inspire people to overcome insurmountable odds...Life is short, so live it out doing something that you care about...Try to make a difference the best way you can. There's an enormous satisfaction in seeing the cultural transformation that happens when an organization is turned on to purpose." writes Roy M. Spence Jr. in It's Not What You Sell, It's What You Stand for.

Remaining true to yourself: April 1945, the Pacific. In the midst of a fierce battle, about eighty war-hardened American soldiers owed their lives to one man, Private Desmond Doss. They once had mocked him for his refusal to carry a gun. However, while enemy crossfire took down soldier after soldier, the medic, Private Doss, ignoring the danger to his life, dragged more than 75 wounded men to safety. The man who was once a butt of their jokes became their hero. Doss was not afraid to stand up for what he believed, and he was not afraid to stand up on the battlefield. For his outstanding bravery, Doss was awarded the Congressional Medal of Honor by the president of the United States.

> **Team Focused**

❖ Am I willing to share my power to ensure the mission is accomplished?

❖ Do I know the aspirations of my team members?

❖ Do I challenge followers to become even better?

There's a branch of philosophy called "ethical egoism," which teaches that each person should look after their interests and ignore the interests of others, except where the interest of others contributes toward his or her own goals. Therefore people should look out for themselves only. That's an attitude which doesn't need to be taught because it's already wired in our genes. Often people who rise to the level of leadership will seize the opportunity to serve themselves without thinking of the people they are leading. The truth is almost anybody once given the opportunity, can spend money or command others. However, it takes true greatness to act the part of a servant and do tasks that others don't want to do. It takes great strength to share your knowledge and mentor and coach others and not consider that they may take your position. It takes true greatness to put others first, to treat others as you want to be treated. Do you strive to be a servant? To whom: to yourself or others? If you don't serve others, in the end, you will ultimately be serving something. Thinking of others more than yourself causes you to uplift, encourage, and appreciate them. Such leaders don't follow material possessions but accept a higher calling. Their focus is on people. They find fulfilment in adding value to the people they lead. Purpose-driven leaders always consider, "how can this benefit the group?" They believe that people have an intrinsic value beyond their tangible contributions as employees. As such, they are deeply committed to the personal and professional growth of every individual within the organization. They keep the goal in hindsight while focusing on their team. Strive to learn as much as possible about your employees. Effective leaders who know their employees' aspirations can link those goals to their work and then enjoy the improved performance that it brings. Purpose-driven leaders meet the current performance goals yet plan for the future as they are always looking ahead. They help others achieve their goals. They are about bringing people together who would work for the common good. Such leaders focus on making more leaders. They train and equip followers to continue the mission so even if they are not there, the work will go on. They raise up a strong team who are highly capable and they rest assured the vision does not die with them.

> **Community / Society Focused**

❖ How can I contribute or how can I give back?

❖ What do I want to be known for?

❖ What is the effect of my leadership efforts on my community?

Alexander the Great first drove the Persians out of Asia Minor. Following his victories at Granicus (334 B.C.) and Issus (333 B.C.), he marched his armies down through Syria, Phoenicia, and Palestine to Egypt, taking time to destroy the kingdoms along the way, including the great sea-power of the island city of Tyre (332-331 B.C.). After defeating Egypt, he turned east and did not rest till he had reached India. He marched his soldiers 10,000 miles in approximately ten years. When he returned to Babylon, he was only 32 years old, and the world was at his feet. Yet, in 323 B.C., at the height of his glory, he died of fever and exhaustion.

Power when used correctly can be a great blessing; for with power one can guide and even command others in the right direction. It's also a very easy thing to abuse. As it is often said, "Absolute power corrupts." Most of us, in one way or another, have authority over others. The question is how do we use it? One of the main characteristics of purpose-driven leadership is the conviction that the well-being of people is the end of leadership and not that people are the means to the leader's goals. Our world doesn't need more numbers centred leaders, but purpose-driven leaders who can help solve real-world problems. "The key challenge for business is how do we get more purpose-driven leaders that realise they are there to make a difference in the world", said Bill George of Harvard Business School. "The pressures are greater today than they've ever been on CEOs to produce short-term results but it's really not about that. It's about having a company that's going to solve actual social problems through the work the company does and that requires a company with commitment to purpose throughout the entire organisation."

Purpose driven leaders seek to understand the realities of the present and the likely consequence of a decision in the future. We need leaders who see the big picture and understand the importance of making contributions to building a better world. If your sole purpose in leading is to accumulate wealth, you may be hugely disappointed. In today's uncertain economic environment the accumulation of material possessions does not guarantee stability or a rewarding life.

The Great Depression began in October 1929, when the stock market in the United States crashed. Thousands of investors lost large sums of money, and bank savings were wiped out; many people lost everything overnight. One wealthy businessman who owned three homes found himself with his family living under a bridge for almost two years; they survived by selling off various belongings. This was a businessman that one year prior had taken a luxurious cruise and an extended vacation in Europe.

Purpose-driven leaders are always on the alert for the next field of service. They work towards building a more sustainable future. People are depending on you, not just internally in the company but externally in the society.

LEADING WITH THE HEART

The heart is considered the centre of all emotions. It is the centre of the will; it designates the inward man, the hidden area of the being. The heart houses our true motives and feelings. From the heart, good and evil thoughts arise, and in the heart, resolutions take shape which determines our destiny. As leaders, we are called to follow a high standard. The wise leader, therefore, guards their heart.

We should therefore, keep our heart, the centre of our whole being with all diligence. *Why* should we keep it that way? Because it is critical to all aspects of our leadership walk.

The war within - Thus, unlike battles fought noisily with guns, tanks, jets, this one happens in silence, in the quiet recesses of the human conscience. The leadership journey is a battle between the old you and the transformed you. No matter how earnestly we seek to walk this leadership road, there will come a point we will have to fight the battle against self, however, as long as we don't lose sight of our guiding principles we will be victorious.

"The Roots Of Our Problems Are: Wealth Without Work, Pleasure Without Conscience, Knowledge Without Character, Commerce Without Morality, Science Without Humanity, Worship Without Sacrifice, Politics Without Principles."— Mahatma Gandhi

The High Calling of Leadership

The road less travelled. Imagine walking along a narrow path. Along the way, there are numerous paths leading in different directions. Some of these paths obviously go to places that we would not want to visit. Others look tempting; they appeal to our emotions, our feelings and our desires. If we take any one of them, we get off the right path and go on a road that might be exceedingly difficult to get off. Temptations can be very difficult because they appeal to things we really want, and they seem to come at our weakest moments. "Two roads diverged in a wood, and I took the one less travelled by, and that has made all the difference." So wrote Robert Frost in his poem "The Road Not Taken." The concept of two roads or gates-- one being broad and appealing (selfishness, pride, dishonesty), the other, narrow and foreboding (self-sacrifice, humility, love). Great leaders take the narrow road. The more we indulge in selfishness, pride, dishonesty, the more difficult it is to perceive the right decision in any given situation. On the contrary, the narrow road can be rewarding but can be very rough, yet it offers us genuine happiness that leaves us with a good taste in this life. We need to strive and press on, leading with purpose in spite of the many setbacks and obstacles faced.

HEART-LED LEADERS VALUE:

GENEROSITY

Just as leaders strive to excel in other virtues, leaders should seek excellence in generosity. A gift is most highly appreciated when it meets a felt need. Generosity is voluntary, not forced. It looks for opportunities to give. Small as well as large organizations can be generous. Generous leaders gave back to their communities and society. They seek out ways to help others. There are prevalent gross inequities in our world today. What would you say about an auction a few years ago in Canada during which someone paid $85,000 for a bottle of 1735 wine from Germany while millions of people don't even have regular access to fresh drinking water? Though the causes of poverty are complex, there's no doubt that greed, selfishness and corruption have made it a lot worse

How should we relate to the needs of, others when their poverty is the result of laziness or bad management? "You can easily judge the character of a man by how he treats those who can do nothing for him."—Malcolm S. Forbes.

Be generous, and give what you have even if it is only a smile or a greeting. A generous person enjoys prosperity. Try to understand the inner needs of each individual you meet. Look beneath the surface. When possible, help others to help themselves. William Booth, co-founder of the Salvation Army, offered "soup, soap, and salvation," in that order. Several years ago an interesting story was published about Mrs Rose Mc Mullin. This woman had been travelling back and forth across America, donating blood everywhere she went. She had just arrived in New York City to give blood to a 25-year-old mother. Not long before that, she had given another transfusion. At the time of the news release, she had supplied more than 300 pints of blood in 40 U.S. States.

COMPASSION

We cannot be truly generous without compassion. The word compassion generally evokes positive feelings. We like to think of ourselves as compassionate people who are primarily good and kind. We identify being compassionate with being truly human. We feel offended when someone accuses us of lacking compassion. The word compassion is derived from Latin words meaning, "to suffer with." Compassion requires us to identify with the weak, hurting, vulnerable, and the powerless. Compassion means complete immersion in the effort to relieve human need. It means taking action. It is more than mere kindness. It is something that often arouses in us deep resistance or even protest when we see others' plight.

In August 2015, the stock market took a plunge raising worry and concern of a global economic fallout that doomsayers had predicted for months. Many news outlets ran stories with the simple message "don't panic." One of those messages caught the attention of Howard Schultz, CEO of Starbucks who emailed all store managers with this note: be extra considerate and kind to your customers today because some are having a bad week. Being compassionate is not about being extra nice and soft and avoiding problems It's about retaining a dignity and respect for humanity. We lead people, not organizations, and our mission is to serve people, not a goal. People are the foundation that make organizational goals happen. Compassionate leadership focuses on connection and community. It gets the job done without sacrificing people in the process. There will always be critics to the compassionate leadership movement. Just minutes after Schultz's email was made public, some criticized his motives and questioned his sincerity.

"If you are kind, people may accuse you of selfish, ulterior motives. Be kind anyway...In the final analysis, it is between you and God. It was never between you and them anyway." —Mother Teresa

PEACE

Finding Peace. On a scale of 1 to 10 (1 is very peaceful, 10 is very anxious), how would you rate your life? People are increasingly frustrated in their search for personal peace. Peace means tranquillity, calmness, restfulness. It is an occurrence of harmony characterized by, lack of violence, conflict behaviours and the freedom from fear of violence. Dr. Robert Oppenheimer, who supervised the creation of the first atomic bomb, appeared before a Congressional Committee in the United States. They inquired of him if there were any defence against the weapon. 'Certainly,' the great physicist replied.

"And that is..."

"Dr. Oppenheimer looked over the hushed, expectant audience and said softly **'Peace.'** "-Compiled by Paul Lee Tan, Encyclopedia of 7,700 Illustrations: Signs of the Times 1988, p. 989.

What is in your heart? Is it getting what you want at all cost? Everything we do has a consequence. Cause and effect always go together. Isaac Newton, as a young man, formulated one of the most basic laws of motion: "For every action, there is an equal and opposite reaction." Second Strike: "He hit me first!" "No! He hit me first—deliberately!" Sounds all too familiar. This logic is not only appealing to children but to leaders and entire nations, as well. A military strike or war is legitimate if it responds to incitement by the other side. Of course, the other side is sure that it was also provoked which leads to cycles of attacks which can go on for years, or even centuries, causing untold suffering.

The world is stirred with the spirit of war. What is the source of fightings and wars? Greed, jealousy, selfishness and hatred, etc. Leaders ideally are instruments of peace. The United Nations sometimes sends its peacekeepers to places where there are uprisings to keep the peace. In a world of war. We need leaders who will make peace; leaders that seek the re-establishing of peace wherever there is conflict. Leaders that value peace will try to still the rough waters for they know in war, no one really wins. Leaders must love justice. Not quick to condemn or place judgement on others. "Peace seems to be an elusive dream for the human race. In 1895 Alfred Nobel, the inventor of dynamite, provided for a trust to establish a prize for individuals who make an outstanding contribution to peace" (Paul Lee Tan, p. 988, adapted). In recent years, however, even some winners of the Nobel Peace Prize have been involved in violent conflicts.

Sometimes Peace is right in front of us if we embrace it. World War II ended in 1945 while a Japanese soldier named Shoichi Yokoi hid in the jungle on the island of Guam. Leaflets dropped from U.S. planes proclaimed peace, but Yokoi thought it a trick. A loyal, patriotic soldier of the emperor, he vowed never to surrender. He had no contact with civilization and lived on what he could find in the jungle. In 1972, 27 years after the end of World War II, hunters came across Yokoi while he was fishing, and he only then learned that the message of peace had been true. While the rest of his people had been enjoying peace for decades, Yokoi had been enduring decades of privation and stress—Roy Gane, Altar Call (Berrien Spring, Mich.: Diadem, 1999)

GOODNESS

Goodness is derived from the Old English word godnes. Thus, it is associated with qualities that are like God. Goodness is character energized, expressing itself in good deeds. A "good heart" is revealed in good deeds and good actions that benefit others. Good intentions, good thoughts are fine, but in the end, goodness is to do good. Jeffrey Immelt of GE once said that "To be a great corporation today, first you have to be a good one." Years ago, Russian writer Fyodor Dostoyevsky wrote a book about his time in a Siberian prison camp, where some of Russia's worst criminals were incarcerated. Among the prisoners were those who had committed some of the most heinous crimes imaginable. Dostoyevsky wrote about how, at times, these men were capable of doing some of the kindest and gentlest acts.

Goodness is love in action. When we have love in our hearts, there will be a positive outflow of goodness to the people with whom we are in contact with. Good means that we look for potential in others. Sadly, though, we do not always look for the best in others. We often tend to see the mistakes others make rather than the things they could do if properly coached and trained. In our relationships with employees, we may primarily focus on their weaknesses rather than to build on their strengths. We should encourage them to strive to be the very best version of themselves. Goodness will lead leaders to manifest understanding and sensitivity toward others and to fight for justice for all. It is hard to see someone being unfairly treated. And it is very painful when we are at the receiving end of such unfair treatment. Because we normally have a strong sense of justice, when we see injustice occurring our instinct is to put things right.

While support for leaders shouldn't be blind—that is, we do whatever they instruct us to do, no questions asked—true support doesn't mean we endorse leaders only when we absolutely agree with everything they do. One of the sad facts of life is that there can be some very charming, charismatic leaders; leaders with great skills and insight whom we often label as "good" when, in fact, they are terrible to the core. Do selfishness or love motivate your kind acts? Do you just want to look good in front of others or do you genuinely care? The word good can, like the word love, be so readily and cheaply thrown around that it loses its true meaning.

The whole world grimaced in horror some years ago when more than 900 men, women and children died in a remote village in Guyana. No weapon or natural disaster killed them. They died because their leader instructed them to drink a deadly poison sweetened by a flavoured drink. Only a few escaped. Investigations made one think clear. Most of the people were not independent thinkers. Sadly, they did exactly what their leader told them to do.

FAITHFULNESS

Faithfulness is displaying dedication to ones cause. Those who are faithful do what they promise to do. Faithfulness speaks of a firmness of purpose and implies steadfast adherence. Synonyms include loyalty, implying a strong allegiance to one's principles or purpose and unwavering determination. It's going beyond emotions to do the acceptable and right thing.

> Faithfulness is demonstrating:

❖ Humility— It's staying down-to-earth regardless of what you've achieved.

❖ Dependability—This means people can count on you. It's bringing the best you to every moment even when you don't feel like it.

❖ Loyalty is devotion. It is standing by someone even when things get tough.

During World War II England, an air raid warden advertisement appeared in the British Newspapers calling for volunteer messengers.

It read: "Boys, 16 and over, to run messages – apply A.R.P. Warden." Derrick Belfall only 14 years, offered his services to his war-ravaged country. He was turned down because of his age. Under regulations, the minimum age for messengers was sixteen. But fourteen-year-old Belfall had been persistent, and his parents and the authorities finally allowed him to serve. During an air raid on December 2, 1940, he was sent with a message, which he delivered. On his return to his post, he passed a house that had caught fire, and he stopped to fight the fire. When the homeowner took over, he continued on his way but heard cries for help. He entered another house where he rescued an injured baby.

With the air raid still underway, he continued back to his post but was injured in an explosion. He was taken to the hospital. When they asked him if he wanted to send a last word to anyone, he murmured, "Just say, Messenger Belfall reporting. I have delivered my message", and then he died. Derrick Cecil Belfall showed great faithfulness. He died on active service aged 14 years.

JOY & HAPPINESS

Joy and happiness are not necessarily the same thing. Happiness is the result of favourable circumstances; joy, in contrast, is the result of doing the right things and being of service to others. Joy is seeing how we inspire others. Happiness is as unpredictable as a harvest. Inward joy is constant; happiness is temporary. Joy is an internal gladness in life that runs deeper than pain or pleasure. Many leaders allow themselves to be held captive by their circumstances and consequently sway between an emotional high and low. For them, to rejoice seems unreasonable, even impossible in the face of poor results. It can take just one email, phone call or report to change your mood. In this uncertain environment you need to be grounded, or else your highs and lows will fluctuate like the stock market. Even when external situations are not ideal, I have joy in my heart which is constant. I choose to maintain a grateful and thankful spirit. Furthermore, many leaders today do not have joy simply because they are self-centred. However real our problems, by focusing solely on them, we only magnify them. About four centuries before Christ, the Greek philosopher Aristotle wrote about "the end," meaning the final purpose of things, he said that the end of humanity, its ultimate purpose, is "happiness"—that which we seek "always for itself and never for the sake of something else."

American author Benjamin Franklin once said that only two things were certain, death and taxes (and though not everyone pays the equivalent taxes, everyone faces death). For many people as they near the end of their lives, they look back and see how vain, how futile, how useless their works were. Reviewing one's past can be discouraging, as in the case of leaders who regretted that their years of service had been unfruitful. The buildings they had built were later destroyed. They wished instead that they had invested more time and energy into developing people. "If only" is a common lament. "If only I had made better decisions in my life!" "If only I had all the facts", "If only I knew then what I know now." A profitable multi-national corporation boasted of high profits in the local newspapers. Yet only four blocks away a woman and her 4-year-old cancer-stricken daughter lived in deplorable conditions. Is this true success? We can't save everybody, but we can make a great impact by doing what we can, even if it is only in a small way.

> **Some of the destructive lies we may come to believe?**

❖ I must have everyone's approval.

❖ The more money I have, the happier I will be.

❖ My job title defines my purpose.

A poster once read, "Money doesn't make you happy, but it sure makes misery a lot more comfortable." Material possessions or having great wealth is not wrong. The danger lies in misplaced priorities. Money can do strange things to people. Things are part of the pleasures of life, but they are not life itself. No matter how many possessions you may have, they never seem to be enough. However, things will rust, break, or hopelessly deteriorate. Sadly too our bodies are not built to last forever. Athletes get injured, beauty queens grow old, and teachers become forgetful. Life is frightfully insecure if based on possessions. Purpose-driven leaders understand the foundation of strong leadership is built on a deeper purpose, greater than yourself. Today there is a widespread lack of confidence in leadership as self-serving behaviours seem to be the norm. Every leader needs to regain and maintain trust. People want genuine leaders who are interested in them and in the community in which they operate. It is never too early or too late to discover your purpose and become a force for social change. Can we expect that our determination to embrace virtues and principles, no matter the cost, will mean that things will turn out okay for us in the short term? Why do bad things happen to good people? Why do rosebuds exist with thorns? What about individuals who have lost their jobs, their spouses or their families, because they preferred to do the right thing? I believe in the long term if not in the short term things will work out for the best. You may be doing a lot of good for others and creating intrinsic value, however, not everyone will cheer you on. Stakeholders may question your position, if they don't agree with the causes you support. Purpose-driven leadership is not about a position, job title, or how much money you make. It's about a heightened level of humility, passion and vision to move others and the world we live in, to a higher level.

LEAVING A LEGACY

"Everything in human life and human history," wrote Reinhold Niebuhr, "moves toward an end."

A GOOD NAME

A name is not a mere label of identification but an expression of its bearer's nature. A good name is a priceless treasure. It increases the effectiveness of our influence. Reputation can be easily destroyed by gossip or slander, but it does not have to destroy the character. Who you really are is of utmost importance, someone once said, "Given the choice between the name of a great company and its tangible assets, I would choose the name." Why? Without the name, the assets could depreciate, whereas the name itself could rebuild the assets lost and then gain even more. In ancient times people attached great significance to personal names. Names were symbolic of the character and personality of the holder and sometimes reflected the moods or feelings of the one giving the name.

A man in the army of Alexander the Great was named Alexander; he was also accused of cowardly actions. He was brought before Alexander, who asked his name. The man replied softly, "Alexander." "I can't hear you," the ruler stated. The man again said, a little louder, "Alexander." The process was repeated one more time, after which Alexander the Great commented, "Either change your name or change your conduct." Names can sometimes be like trademarks. They become so closely associated with certain characteristics that when we hear the name, we immediately recall these traits. What traits come to mind, when you think of these names: Mother Teresa, Nelson Mandela, Abraham Lincoln, Martin Luther King, Jr., and Mahatma Gandhi?

HOW WILL YOU MEASURE YOUR LIFE?

"Perhaps the ultimate test of a leader is not what you are able to do in the here and now - but instead what continues to grow long after you're gone" —Tom Rath. Leaders are concerned about their legacy, whatever it is. How depressing to think that you worked so hard all your life to build up something, only to have someone come after and bring it to nothing. Alfred Nobel invented dynamite, which he sold for use in mining, railroading, and other construction—creating safer, more efficient labour. But the military soon discovered its destructive power in wartime. Not wanting to be remembered for a weapon that caused so much destruction, Alfred made sure that the bulk of his estate would go to fund humanitarian advances in science, peace, and medicine—we know these awards as a "Nobel Prize."

According to Nelson Henderson, "the true meaning of life is to plant trees under whose shade you do not expect to sit."

Russian author Leo Tolstoy once wrote to a friend that "Once a man has realized that death is the end of everything, then there is nothing worse than life either." Research shows that without a sense of working to create a legacy, we lose meaning in life. The sun rises and sets, the wind blows, the rivers flow, and it goes on and on for generation after generation. Frenchman Jean-Paul Sartre argued that a person's life is basically defined by that person's death, in the sense that at death it's finished. No more changes; no more growth. Everybody wants to be happy, yet, few know how to achieve it. Our world offers all sorts of enticements that promise happiness but always prove in the end to be shallow, fleeting, and empty. One of the most famous, and successful, businessmen in American history was Lee Iacocca, who ran the giant Chrysler Corporation for many years. Toward the end of his life, he once said, "Here I am in the twilight years of my life, still wondering what it's all about. . . . I can tell you this, fame and fortune is for the birds."

Legacy is about building for the future, but it also requires learning from the past. If we don't leave a positive legacy, what kind of society are we creating? What kind of world are we leaving behind? What are we passing on to our future generations? Legacy may remind us of death, but it's not about death. It's about life and the choices we make. However, being reminded of death may not be a bad thing, because it gives us a perspective on what's important. Thinking about our legacy helps us decide the kind of life we want to live and the heritage we want to leave behind. It means developing and passing on a timeless part of ourselves. The idea of leaving something meaningful behind that will live forever is appealing. We all hope to be remembered in some way after we're gone, to have what we've done and held dear to live on after us. We also want to feel that our lives matter and in the vast sea of humanity we could leave footprints. Most of us will not be a Nelson Mandela, with our name and achievements remembered forever in the history books. In reality, if you don't pass on your life experience by leaving a legacy, the wisdom you've gained will disappear after you leave this earth.

Human beings possess a craving for immortality. A well-known magazine ran a full-page advertisement with a headline that read: Achieve Immortality! The poster went on to say; you can leave a charitable legacy that will make gifts in your name forever. Writers, scholars, philosophers, and theologians through the millennia have all grappled with the question of death and what it does to the meaning of our lives. Hence, the advertisement was an amusing, way to help people deal with their mortality. One of the very best ways to achieve a meaningful legacy is to actively engage yourself and others in thoughtful philanthropy while you live. The important question we should ask ourselves is, "what kind of world do I want to live in, and what can I do to make this happen so that a 100 or 200 years from now, this world will be better place not just for my descendants but for all."

Your life at this moment - A primary challenge of human beings is making choices about the present, but with the awareness of an uncertain future. If you don't have a life map, you end up drifting around hopelessly lost. No one can survive living simply from moment to moment, ignoring the future. Johann Wolfgang von Goethe said "Choose well. Your choice is brief and yet endless."

BEARING GOOD FRUIT

Good Fruit can only come out of healthy leadership. Fruit represents something in the process of growth, maturity or even decay. Fruit can be sweet, pleasant or sour. We should strive to bear good fruit. Without having love in our hearts for others, we cannot produce genuine fruit, just as a branch cannot bear fruit unless it is connected to the vine. In the same way, a leader filled with the heart of love will care about others. Good fruit is the natural product of putting others before ourselves. What is your greatest accomplishment ever? Life goes by so fast.

Ulrich was in his early fifties and working as a CEO of a very successful company. In December 1998, He noticed that a large mole on his back. He immediately went to his doctor to have it removed. The doctor requested a biopsy be firstly done but he refused. Everything seemed all right after the surgery. A year later Ulrich saw three tiny moles on the scar of his first surgery. He returned to his physician, this time the pathology report confirmed he had melanoma, a cancer of the skin. Ulrich's doctor told him that he could expect to live only a few years. His world crumbled. He did not mention his diagnosis to anyone. He was divorced and didn't want to worry his elderly parents or children. After Ulrich was released from the hospital, he made the decision to turn around his life completely. The things that he thought were so important didn't seem to matter anymore. Previously his focus was solely on the bottom line, but now it was on the people who made the bottom line possible. He invested more time in doing good for others and in serving the community. The community is vital to remembering the past and fulfilling responsibilities to the future. Ulrich was declared cancer-free by his doctor after three years of being diagnosed, but the scare was a good wake up call for him to take stock of his life and to shift focus to what really matters. He concentrated on his legacy. He moved away from the selfish culture he had promoted and sought to teach and trains others thus steering the organization towards a culture which valued teamwork. On the path to delivering results, he realized the journey was about forming meaningful relationships and bringing people together to work for the common goal. He found balance and real meaning in life and became a model of true leadership. As Tavis Smiley stated, "The choices we make about the lives we live determine the kinds of legacies we leave." Live a life that you can smile and feel a deep sense of fulfilment when you reflect.

Conclusion

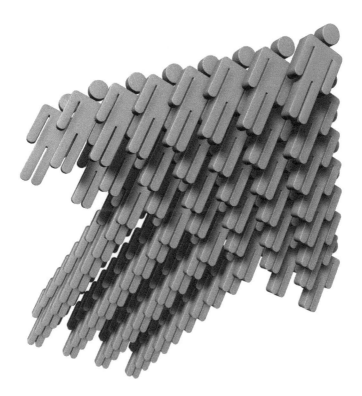

Great leaders understand that they are only as good as their weakest link so they build a powerful network of teams who are committed to the vision. They train, coach and mentor others. They are interested in the growth of their team and in making more leaders. Where teamwork abounds, people are engaged, motivated, and want to be part of the winning team and this is the culture leaders should strive to maintain in their organizations. It will have a tremendous impact on your productivity and overall bottom line. Purpose Driven Leaders work with a purpose and encourage others to do so. They make a positive impact which is not only felt in the present but also in the future.

References

Austin, W. J. (2009). Strategic planning for smart leadership: Rethinking your organization's collective future through a workbook-based, three-level model (2nd Ed.).Stillwater, OK: New Forums Press.

Bass B.M. (1990) From transactional to transformational leadership: learning to share the vision. Organisational Dynamics 18, 19–31.

Burns, J. (1978). Leadership. New York, NY: Harper and Row.

Elena, Holodny. (2015). Article Title. China's GDP is expected to surpass the US' in 11 years, http://www.businessinsider.com/chinas-gdp-is-expected-to-surpass-the-us-in-11-years-2015-6.

Fitzsimmons, S. R. (2013). Multicultural employees: A framework for understanding how they contribute to organizations. Academy of Management Review, 38, *525-549*. doi:10.5465/amr.2011.0234

Hall, J., Johnson, S., Wysocki, A. & Kepner, K. (2002). Transformational leadership: the transformation of managers and associates. Retrieved August 3, 2006

http://www.mckinsey.com/business-functions/organization/our-insights/why-diversity-matters

http://www.gallup.com/poll/193901/employee-engagement-steady-june.aspx

http://www.diversityinc.com/the-diversityinc-top-50-companies-for-diversity-2016/

Journal of Management, 28: 517–543. Mahoney, T. A. 1988. Productivity defined: The relativity of efficiency, effectiveness, and change. In J. P. Campbell & R. J. Campbell (Eds.), Productivity in organizations: 13– 39. San Francisco: Jossey-Bass.

McEachern, M. (2005). Understanding inspiration and inspirational leadership in the workplace informs leadership practices and transformational results. Masters Abstracts International, 44, 01.

Matsumoto, D. (1996). Culture and psychology. Pacific Grove, CA: Brooks/Cole Publishing Company.

Northouse P.G. (2004) Leadership: Theory and Practice, 3rd edn. Sage Publications, London

Sean Wise (Ryerson University) Article Title "Can a Team Have Too Much Cohesion? The Dark Side to Network Density," by, *European Management Journal*, Oct. 2014, vol. 32, no. 5

Statistic Times and the International Monetary Fund (2016). http://statisticstimes.com/economy/countries-by-projected-gdp.php

Epilogue

‖‖‖

We have come to the end of this book. Thank you for staying with it. I hope you have known at all times that the author has your best interests in mind. **Purpose Driven Leadership: Building and Fostering Effective Teams** gives strategies for increasing employee engagement, commitment and subsequent productivity. It combines wisdom from the ages with the author's insights; thus, giving a winning formula for success.

May you apply these principles outlined in this book to foster a high performance culture of Teamwork in your organization. It has worked for many others and can do exactly the same for you.

I wish you the very best in life!

Sincerely,
Brigette

Notes